Starting Lines
Beginning Writing

David Blot

Bronx Community College
City University of New York

David M. Davidson

Bronx Community College
City University of New York

Heinle & Heinle Publishers
I T P® An International Thomson Publishing Company

Pacific Grove • Albany • Bonn • Boston • Cincinnati • Detroit • London • Madrid • Melbourne
Mexico City • New York • Paris • San Francisco • Tokyo • Toronto • Washington

Heinle & Heinle Publishers
20 Park Plaza
Boston, MA 02116 U.S.A.

International Thomson
* Publishing*
Berkshire House 168-173
High Holborn
London WC1V7AA
England

Thomas Nelson Australia
102 Dodds Street
South Melbourne, 3205
Victoria, Australia

Nelson Canada
1120 Birchmont Road
Scarborough, Ontario
Canada M1K5G4

International Thomson
* Publishing Gmbh*
Königwinterer Strasse 418
53227 Bonn
Germany

International Thomson
* Publishing Asia*
221 Henderson Road
* No. 05–10*
Henderson Building
Singapore 0315

International Thomson
* Publishing–Japan*
Hirakawacho-cho Kyowa
* Building, 3F*
2-2-1 Hirakawacho-cho
Chiyoda-ku, 102 Tokyo
Japan

The publication of *Starting Lines* was directed by the members of the Newbury House Publishing Team at Heinle & Heinle:

Erik Gundersen, Editorial Director
John McHugh, Market Development Director
Kristin Thalheimer, Production Services Coordinator
Elizabeth Holthaus, Director of Production and Team Leader

Also participating in the publication of this program were:

Publisher: Stanley J. Galek
Project Manager: J. Carey Publishing Service
Assistant Editor: Karen P. Hazar
Associate Production Editor: Maryellen Eschmann
Manufacturing Coordinator: Mary Beth Hennebury
Interior Designer: Carla Bolte
Cover Designer: Bortman Design Group
Photo Coordinator: Maryellen Eschmann

Photo Credits
(Lesson) 1—Jonathan Stark-Heinle & Heinle/2—Superstock/3—Jean-Claude LeJeune-Stock, Boston/4—Ulrike Welsch/5—Ulrike Welsch-Photo Edit/6—Gary A. Conner-Photo Edit/7—Amy Etra-Photo Edit/8—Charles Duprez-Brown Brothers/9—Jonathan Stark-Heinle & Heinle/10—Michael Lajoie Photography/11—Michael Lajoie Photography/12—John Maher-Stock, Boston/13—Author/14—Michael Lajoie Photography/15—Michael Lajoie Photography/16—Gale Zucker-Stock, Boston/17—Superstock/18—Michael Dwyer-Stock, Boston/19—Stacy Pick-Stock, Boston/20—Jonathan Stark-Heinle & Heinle/21—Superstock/22—Robert Brenner-Photo Edit/23—Jean-Claude LeJeune-Stock, Boston/24—Judy Gelles-Stock, Boston/25—Stephen McBrady-Photo Edit/26—Freeman/Grishaber-Photo Edit/27—Jerry Howard-Stock, Boston/28—Uniphoto Picture Agency/29—Olive R. Pierce-Stock, Boston/30—Hazel Hankin-Stock, Boston

Library of Congress Cataloging in Publication Data
Blot, Dave.
    Starting lines / David Blot, David M. Davidson.
       p.   cm.
    ISBN 0-8384-5258-2
    1. English language—Textbooks for foreign speakers.
    I. Davidson, David M.   II. Title.
    PE1128.B5935   1995
    428.2'4 — dc20   94-39153
                                                                CIP

Heinle & Heinle Publishers is a division of International Thomson Publishing, Inc.

Manufactured in the United States of America.
ISBN 0-8384-5258-2
10 9 8 7 6 5 4 3 2 1

Contents

SECTION TWO　　SUPPLEMENTARY PARAGRAPHS　　127

The tasks in this section provide students with further practice in achieving coherent and accurate writing. To expand upon materials taught in Lessons 1–30, students are asked to restructure existing paragraphs by manipulating pronoun references, verb tenses, and other grammatical features.

Checksheet for Supplementary Paragraphs　**129**

SECTION THREE   GRAMMAR PAGES   155

SECTION FOUR   HANDWRITING PRACTICE   173

Following a Thematic Approach

Many instructors will choose to follow the lessons in the order in which they are presented. These lessons build gradually, one upon the other, in grammatical complexity. Other instructors—those who follow a more thematic approach—may choose to reorder the lessons in the following groupings:

1. *Home*

Lessons

Supplementary Paragraphs

2. *School*

Lessons

Supplementary Paragraphs

3. *Work*

Lessons

Supplementary Paragraphs

Introduction

Starting Lines is for the "beginning" English as a Second Language (ESL) student,

- **one who has almost no knowledge of English,** or
- **one who has enough speaking and reading ability for day-to-day living, but who cannot function in an academic environment,** or
- **anyone in between.**

Starting Lines is for the "adult" student. "Adult" **can** mean an ESL student

- **in the 11th or 12th grade of high school,** or
- **in a community or four-year college program,** or
- **in an adult education program.**

But "adult" **must** mean a student who is mature enough to attempt to talk and write about real-life issues, and who is prepared to take considerable responsibility for her/his own learning.

A COMPLETE SKILLS PROGRAM

Starting Lines is the first in a series of three textbooks designed to promote effective writing. Our complete writing program includes the following:

- *Starting Lines* . . . Beginning
- *Write from the Start* . . . High beginning
- *Put it in Writing* . . . Intermediate

PEDAGOGICAL APPROACH

Starting Lines uses a holistic approach to the teaching of English, combining observation, reading, discussion, and writing activities to assist the student in the development of basic English competency. Our expectation is that at the end of a semester-long course using this text (with additional reading, grammar, and writing exercises as appropriate), a student will be able to demonstrate:

a) clarity and accuracy of form in writing, including legibility, punctuation, paragraphing, and use of margins.

b) a knowledge of basic English sentence structure in writing paragraphs with considerable accuracy in the use of:
   simple present, past, future, and present continuous tenses

subject and object pronouns and possessive adjectives
plurals/articles/infinitives/modals

c) comprehension of simple reading passages through oral and written responses.

Our further expectation is that students will enjoy learning to write through interaction with stimulating reading that promotes thinking, discussion, and shared writing activities of different kinds.

We also expect students to feel more comfortable with the process of learning English and with the self-responsibility that this learning entails.

In short, our goal is to help develop an individual who is ready for more advanced ESL study, and who can participate more fully in our society with improved communication in English.

The Paragraphs

Each of the 30 lessons in *Starting Lines* is centered around a short paragraph with an underdeveloped or understated story line or issue. This understated nature of the paragraphs, accompanied by the illustrations, encourages students to respond to the thematic content through discussion and writing. Thus, while in one activity of each lesson, students are asked to manipulate the core paragraph as a way of recognizing, practicing, and assimilating some aspect of grammar or usage, the focus of the lessons as a whole remains on the content. This focus can also be maintained in the additional paragraphs in the second part of the book. Students are referred to these supplementary paragraphs for further grammatical practice. However, an instructor who wishes to follow a thematic approach may choose to refer students to appropriate paragraphs as listed in the table of contents, asking students to react to the accompanying questions rather than, or in addition to, the grammatical concern.

Fluency and Accuracy

Starting Lines offers students the opportunity for a considerable amount of writing. They need to see that even at fairly beginning levels they can write more than they believe they can and that they are not bound by the space limitations on the pages of this book. As students progress in the course, they should be encouraged to write longer pieces, using the space provided in the book only as "starting lines," and continuing to write on their own paper if more space is needed. As they write longer pieces, and use more of their own paper to complete assignments, they will have visible evidence of their increasing fluency. This encouragement and motivation for production, balanced by the instructor's demand for correctness, will help students reach their potential. In our experience, fluency and accuracy go hand-in-hand in the development of an effective communicator.

Vocabulary

Our respect for student abilities and differences determines our approach to vocabulary. Following every core paragraph, students are asked to identify any words or phrases that are unfamiliar to them. With the help of a dictionary (bilingual or English), a classmate, or the instructor (as last resort), the student is expected to write an appropriate synonym or short definition. Because vocabulary is best learned in a communicative context, students are more likely to retain and use the words and phrases that they are reading and writing.

ORGANIZATION OF THE BOOK

A few words about the organization of *Starting Lines* and suggestions for use. For convenience, the paragraphs have been arranged according to the tense they are written in. Where a change of tense is required, the paragraph is grouped with the new tense. For example, a present tense paragraph requiring a change to the past such as "Living Alone" (Lesson 18) is grouped with the past tense paragraphs. In some cases the tense may be irrelevant to the grammatical point in question. You will therefore find paragraphs focusing on pronouns in both the present and past tense sections. (See Lesson 16 "A Disabled Person" and Lesson 23 "A Serious Conversation.")

While most of the additional exercises in the "Present Tense" section call for writing in that tense, a couple of past tense activities are introduced when they seem appropriate to the content. (See Lessons 11 "A Noisy Neighbor" and 12 "Summer Camp.") Similarly, the limited use of possessive adjectives is called for (also in Lesson 12) before students have had the opportunity to deal with them in a structured paragraph. While we have been mindful of "sequencing," our experience indicates that student abilities often outpace our "lessons" and we are inclined to give such students the opportunity to demonstrate these abilities. Of course, any exercise deemed too difficult can be considered optional.

The first few lessons of *Starting Lines* ask students to copy paragraphs, the purpose being to stress accuracy and attention to detail without an immediate concern for grammar. This activity will give the instructor the opportunity to determine which students need additional work with handwriting and more attention to mechanics. Requiring students to completely rewrite any paragraph with even a single uncorrected error encourages such attention.

To provide guidance and models for activities in the book, we have included a section for handwriting practice, a sample letter and dialogue, and practice grammar sheets for the major grammatical forms presented.

STUDENT RESPONSIBILITY

Many of the exercises are designed for work with a group or a partner. This type of interaction gives students more opportunity to practice the language in a more secure environment and to share their knowledge with each other. Student interaction requires active participation of the instructor (as monitor and advisor) and considerable structure, especially at the beginning of the course. One such structured activity can be the proofreading of each other's rewritten paragraphs. In this way, students can be held responsible for both their own work and that of a partner, thereby promoting accuracy and improving proofreading skills.

The emphasis in our approach is for students to take considerable responsibility for their own learning. They are expected to engage in cooperative group tasks such as discussions, dialogue writing and shared writing, and to work independently when appropriate as in letter writing, vocabulary development, and with the suggested **Additional Activities** at the end of each lesson. Of course, students are also expected to take responsibility for legibility and for standard writing procedures such as paragraphing, the use and placement of titles, and respect for margins.

In conclusion, we believe that a student will learn best when there is inner motivation. And we feel that the best way to motivate students is to involve them in the communicative process. If they are asked to deal with the content of the paragraphs in *Starting Lines*, and to explore the relevance of the issues to their own lives, students will be more likely to show a concern for, and growth in, the handling of English grammar and mechanics.

We wish you and your students success, and trust that *Starting Lines* will be a valuable asset in your work.

David Blot
David M. Davidson

To my beloved wife
PASTORA
and our loveable children
JASON, SHEILA, and JENNIFER
—David Blot

To
KAY, DEBORAH, and DANIEL
with love and appreciation
—David M. Davidson

Lessons

LESSON 1

Our English Teacher

Study page 157 before you do this lesson.

ACTIVITY A   Work with your group or a partner.

1. What is the name of your English teacher? _____

2. How many hours a week do you study English with your teacher? _____

3. What kinds of English activities do you do in your English class? _____

   Example: _____writing_____

   _____   _____   _____

   _____   _____   _____

4. Which is your favorite English activity? _____

5. Does your teacher give you homework assignments? _____

6. How many hours of homework do you do each night? _____

ACTIVITY B   *Read about an English teacher named Ms. Grossman.*

Our English Teacher

Ms. Grossman is our English teacher. She teaches reading and writing. She is a good teacher. She speaks slowly and she explains everything carefully. However, she gives us too much homework. She says that we have to work hard to learn English. We like Ms. Grossman, but we don't like all the homework.

ACTIVITY C   *List each word or phrase in the paragraph that you don't understand. Then find the meaning and write it next to the word or phrase.*

_____   _____

_____   _____

_____   _____

ACTIVITY D   *Copy the paragraph in Activity B. Copy the title also.*

ACTIVITY E   *Change the paragraph in Activity B.*

Ms. Grossman has to stop teaching for a few months because she is going to have a baby. Mr. Levine is the new English teacher. Write about Mr. Levine. Begin your paragraph this way:

Our English Teacher

Mr. Levine is our English teacher. He teaches

ACTIVITY F   *Compare two English teachers.*

List the ways that your English teacher is similar to Ms. Grossman or Mr. Levine.

Example: Ms. / Mr. _____ teaches reading and writing.
                              (your teacher's name)

1. _____
2. _____
3. _____
4. _____

ADDITIONAL ACTIVITY

Do paragraph 1 on page 131.

LESSON 2

The Old Bus

Study page 158 before you do this lesson.

ACTIVITY A   *Work with your group or a partner.*

1. List the different kinds of transportation available in your city or town.

   Example: _____ taxi _____

   _____   _____   _____

   _____   _____   _____

2. Which kind of transportation is the best in your city or town? _____

3. How do you get to school? _____

4. Are the buses in your city or town in good condition? _____

5. How much does it cost to ride on a bus? _____

ACTIVITY B   *Read about the old bus.*

The Old Bus

The bus is old. It is very slow. It is never on time. It is always crowded. In the summer, it is too hot. In the winter, it is too cold. It is always breaking down. Maybe the city will take the bus out of service.

ACTIVITY C   *List each word or phrase in the paragraph that you don't understand. Then find the meaning and write it next to the word or phrase.*

_____   _____

_____   _____

_____   _____

ACTIVITY D   *Copy the paragraph in Activity B. Copy the title also.*

ACTIVITY E   *Change the paragraph in Activity B.*

There are many old buses in the city. Write about these old buses. Begin your paragraph this way:

The Old Buses

The buses are old. They are very

ACTIVITY F   *Write sentences.*

Write five sentences that describe the buses in your city or town.

Example: The buses are old. (or) The buses are new.

1. _____

2. _____

3. _____

4. _____

5. _____

ADDITIONAL ACTIVITY

Do paragraphs 5 and 6 on page 133.

8

LESSON 3

A Good Student

Study page 159 before you do this lesson.

ACTIVITY A   *Work with your group or a partner.*

1. What time does your class start? _____

2. What time do you usually come to class? _____

3. How many times have you come to class late? _____

4. What materials do you bring with you for the class?

    Example: _____a notebook_____

    _____   _____   _____

    _____   _____   _____

5. Do you complete all your homework assignments? _____

6. Do you think you are going to pass your English class? _____

7. What grade do you think you will get? _____

ACTIVITY B   *Read about a good student named Peter.*

A Good Student

Peter is a good student. He is on time for class every day. He is prepared for each class. He is interested in learning English. He is motivated to study and do all the homework. He is going to pass this course.

ACTIVITY C   *List each word or phrase in the paragraph that you don't understand. Then find the meaning and write it next to the word or phrase.*

_____   _____

_____   _____

_____   _____

ACTIVITY D   *Copy the paragraph in Activity B. Copy the title also.*

ACTIVITY E   *Change the paragraph in Activity B.*

There is a student in Peter's class named Sarah. Sarah is not a good student. Write the paragraph in Activity B again, but write about Sarah, not Peter. Begin your paragraph this way:

An Unmotivated Student

Sarah is not a good student. She

ACTIVITY F   *List the ways you demonstrate to your teacher that you are motivated to learn English.*

Example: I do all my homework.

1. I _____

2. I _____

3. I _____

4. I _____

5. I _____

6. I _____

ACTIVITY G   *Write about yourself.*

Put a circle around the title that describes you as a student:

A Good Student   An Unmotivated Student

Use the paragraph in Activity B and write about yourself. Include a title. Begin your paragraph this way:

	[TITLE]
	I am a good student. (or) I am not a good student.

ADDITIONAL ACTIVITY

Do paragraph 8 on page 134.

LESSON 4

My Spouse

> *Study page 157 before you do this lesson.*

ACTIVITY A   *Work with your group or a partner.*

The man and woman in the picture are husband and wife. Their names are Harry and Lucy. They love each other, but Harry complains that Lucy is dull and boring and always follows the same routine. Lucy says the same things about Harry. List some more things that people who live together complain about.

Example: He/She always prepares the same food.

   He/She watches sports on television every weekend.

1. _____

2. _____

3. _____

4. _____

5. _____

ACTIVITY B   *A woman is complaining about her husband. Read what she says about him.*

My Husband

My husband is completely predictable. He always does the same things. He goes to bed at exactly the same time each night. He gets up at exactly the same time each morning. Every Thursday evening he goes out with friends. He stays home every Sunday. He always wears the same style clothes. He never talks about anything except money, work, and the weather. What a life!

ACTIVITY C   *List each word or phrase in the paragraph that you don't understand. Then find the meaning and write it next to the word or phrase.*

_____   _____

_____   _____

_____   _____

ACTIVITY D   *Change the paragraph in Activity B.*

A man is complaining about his wife. Begin your paragraph this way:

My Wife

My wife is completely predictable. She always

ACTIVITY E   *Complete the following sentences about someone you live with.*

1. *My* _____ *is* _____

2. *He/She always* _____

3. *She/He goes to bed* _____

4. *He/She gets up* _____

5. *In the evening he/she* _____

6. *On weekends she/he* _____

7. *He/She always wears* _____

8. *She/He never talks about anything except* _____

_____

ACTIVITY F   *Write a paragraph about someone you live with or someone you know. Include a title. Begin this way:*

	[TITLE]
	My _____ is _____ _____
	He/She

ACTIVITY G   *Make a list of the things you like about a person you live with.*

Examples: He/She cleans up after himself/herself.
He/She shares everything with me.

Things I Like about _____

1. _____
2. _____
3. _____
4. _____
5. _____

ACTIVITY H   *Write a paragraph about a person you live with. Tell about the things you like about the person. Include a title.*

[TITLE]

ADDITIONAL ACTIVITY

Do paragraph 2 on page 131.

LESSON 5

Are You The One?

Study pages 124 and 159 before you do this lesson.

ACTIVITY A   *Work with your group or a partner.*

1. The young man and woman in the picture are happy being together. Make a list of some words that describe the qualities they like about each other.

   Example: <u>understanding</u>   <u>loving</u>   <u>handsome</u>

   _____   _____   _____

   _____   _____   _____

2. Write the things they are saying to each other.

   Example: <u>I love you because you are understanding.</u>

   a. _____

   b. _____

   c. _____

   d. _____

   e. _____

ACTIVITY B   *A man and a woman are thinking about each other and their relationship. Read what one of them says to the other:*

You Are the One

You are kind to me when I need your help. You are sweet to me when I need your kisses. You are loving when I need your love. You are there when I need your understanding. You are everything to me. You are the one that I love most in all the world.

ACTIVITY C   *List each word or phrase in the paragraph that you don't understand. Then find the meaning and write it next to the word or phrase.*

_____   _____

_____   _____

_____   _____

ACTIVITY D   *Change the paragraph in Activity B.*

A man and woman are thinking about each other and their relationship. One of them decides that the other is *not* a good partner. Make all the statements *negative*. Begin your paragraph this way:

You Are Not the One

You are not kind to me when I need your help.

ACTIVITY E   *Answer the questions.*

1. Write the name of a person you love. _____

2. Tell your partner or group why you love this person.

3. Complete the sentences:

   a. *I love you because you* _____

   b. *I also love you because you* _____

   c. *I need you because you* _____

   d. *You are important to me because* _____

ACTIVITY F   *Write a letter to the person you love.*

Tell the reasons for your love. You may use the sentences in Activity E to help you write your letter.

Dear   ,

    You are the person I love the most. I love you

because

ACTIVITY G   *Complete the sentences.*

1. Write the name of a person you don't like. _____

2. Tell your partner or group why you don't like this person.

3. Complete the following sentences:

   a. *I don't like you because you aren't* _____

   b. *Also, you aren't* _____

   c. *I don't need you because you aren't* _____

   d. *You aren't important to me because* _____

ACTIVITY H   *Write a letter to a person you do not like and who wants to see you.*

Tell the reasons you do not want to see him/her. You may use the sentences in Activity G to help you.

Dear _____,
        I don't want to see you. I don't like you because

ADDITIONAL ACTIVITY

Do paragraphs 9 and 10 on page 135.

LESSON 6

The Test

Study pages 157 and 158 before you do this lesson.

ACTIVITY A   *Work with your group or a partner.*

1. The woman in the picture is studying for a test. Make a list of the kinds of tests she might be studying for.

   Example: __History__   _____   _____

   _____   _____   _____

   _____   _____   _____

2. List the ways that people feel when they are preparing for a test.

   Example: __nervous__   _____   _____

   _____   _____   _____

   _____   _____   _____

ACTIVITY B   *Read about two people.*

Janet and Lisa are young women who have an appointment to take a driving test. The following paragraph tells us how they feel.

The Driving Test

Janet and Lisa are nervous. They have a driving test today. They are very worried. They are not sure that they can pass. They are not ready for the test. They are not confident. They are afraid of the examiner. Maybe Janet and Lisa should wait for another day.

ACTIVITY C   *List each word or phrase in the paragraph that you don't understand. Then find the meaning and write it next to the word or phrase.*

_____   _____

_____   _____

_____   _____

ACTIVITY D   *Change the paragraph in Activity B.*

Imagine that only Janet is scheduled to take a driving test today. Write about Janet. Begin your paragraph this way:

Janet's Driving Test

Janet is nervous. She has

ACTIVITY E   *Ask another student in your class these questions. Write the answers.*

1. When is your next test?_____

2. What kind of test is it? _____

3. Are you nervous/anxious/confident/ about this test? _____

4. How many hours each day/week do you study or practice for it? _____

5. Are you ready for the test? _____

6. Are you sure you can pass the test? _____

ACTIVITY F   *Write about a test that one of your classmates has to take. Use the answers to the questions above. Begin your paragraph this way:*

[TITLE]

_____ has a/an _____ test on

_____. She/He is _____ about

the test. He/She _____

ACTIVITY G   *Write a paragraph about Ana and Susan.*

Tell about their next test. When is it? What kind of test is it? Are they nervous, anxious, or confident? Are they ready for the test? Are they sure they can pass the test?

	[TITLE]

ADDITIONAL ACTIVITIES

1. Do paragraphs 3 and 7 on pages 132 and 134.

2. Write a letter to a friend or relative telling about a test you have to take. Tell when you have to take the test, the kind of test it is, how you feel about the test, and how many hours you study for the test. Are you ready for the test? Are you sure you can pass?

LESSON 7

A Helpful Friend

> *Study page 163 before you do this lesson.*

ACTIVITY A   *Work with your group or a partner.*

1. List subjects that are difficult for some students.

   Example: ____math____   _____   _____

   _____   _____   _____

   _____   _____   _____

2. List the subjects that are difficult for you now or were difficult for you when you were younger.

   _____   _____   _____

   _____   _____   _____

3. Who helps you now when you need help with your English or some other subject?

4. In the past who helped you with the subjects that were difficult for you?

ACTIVITY B   *Now read about two helpful friends.*

Helpful Friends

Evelyn and Susan help me with my math homework. They explain the problems to me. They tell me the rules. They show me how to get the right answers. They work with me carefully and patiently. Evelyn and Susan help me in two ways. They teach me math. They give me more confidence in myself.

ACTIVITY C   *List each word or phrase in the paragraph that you don't understand. Then find the meaning and write it next to the word or phrase.*

_____   _____

_____   _____

_____   _____

ACTIVITY D   *Change the paragraph in Activity B.*

Imagine that Susan moved to another city and only Evelyn helps the person in Activity B with his/her math. Write about Evelyn. Begin your paragraph this way:

A Helpful Friend

Evelyn helps me

ACTIVITY E   *Complete the sentences.*

1. *Sometimes I need help with* _____

2. *When I need help, I* _____

3. *I like to help people when* _____

4. *I help* _____ *with* _____

ACTIVITY F   *Write a paragraph.*

Write about a person who helps you in some aspect of your life. What does this person do? How do you feel about this person? Why? Be sure to include a title.

	[TITLE]
	Sometimes I need help with _____. When I
	need help,

ACTIVITY G   *Write a paragraph.*

Write about a person that you help in some way. When do you help this person? What do you do to help this person? How does this person feel about your help? Be sure to include a title.

	[TITLE]
	I help _____ when

ADDITIONAL ACTIVITIES

1. Do paragraphs 11, 12, and 13 on pages 136 and 137.

2. Write a letter to family members or relatives who do not live with you. Tell them about a person who helps you with something, such as school work or child care or household expenses.

LESSON 8

My Desire

Study page 162 before you do this lesson.

ACTIVITY A   *Write the answers to the following questions and then discuss them with your partner or group.*

1. Who are the people in the photograph? _____

2. List some of the things that they might be thinking.

    Example: I am happy to be here. _____

    a. *I am* _____

    b. _____

    c. _____

3. List some of the reasons people come to the United States from other countries.

    Example: To have better job opportunities. _____

    a. *To* _____

    b. _____

    c. _____

ACTIVITY B   *Read about one person's thoughts and feelings.*

My Desire

I like the United States. I like American people. I think American culture is interesting. I want to live here. I want to get a good education. I want to have a good job. I intend to bring the rest of my family here. I want to stay here for the rest of my life.

ACTIVITY C   *List each word or phrase in the paragraph that you don't understand. Then find the meaning and write it next to the word or phrase.*

_____   _____

_____   _____

_____   _____

ACTIVITY D   *Change the paragraph in Activity B.*

Imagine that the person speaking does not like the United States. Begin your paragraph this way.

My Desire

I don't like the United States.

ACTIVITY D   *Tell your partner or group one thing you like and one thing you don't like about the United States. Then write the reasons below. You may talk about any of the following or choose your own topic.*

weather   television   education opportunities
music   movies   job opportunities
clothing   family life   political system
the education system

Example: I like the political system because you can choose your own leaders.

1. *I like* _____ because:

   a. _____

   b. _____

   c. _____

   d. _____

Example: I don't like the weather in the United States because it is too cold in the winter.

2. *I don't like* _____ because:

   a. _____

   b. _____

   c. _____

   d. _____

ACTIVITY F   *Write about something you like in the United States. Tell why you like it.*

	[TITLE]

ACTIVITY G   *Write about something in the United States that you don't like. Tell why you don't like it.*

	[TITLE]

ADDITIONAL ACTIVITIES

1. Do paragraphs 16 and 17 on pages 138 and 139.

2. Write a paragraph about each of the following:

   a. Do you want to bring the rest of your family here? Give your reasons.

   b. Do you want to stay here for the rest of your life? Give your reasons.

LESSON 9

A Job

Study page 162 before you do this lesson.

ACTIVITY A   *Work with your group or a partner.*

1. What kind of job does this person have?

   Example: ___She is an employment counselor.___

   a. *She is* _____

   b. *She works* _____

2. List some of the things that she does each day.

   Example: ___She helps people find jobs.___

   a. *She* _____

   b. *She* _____

3. Tell some of the reasons why she likes the job.

4. What kind of education and training does a person need for this job? A high school diploma? A college degree? Vocational training? On-the-job training? Explain.

ACTIVITY B   *Read about Ana's job.*

A Good Job

Ana has a good job. She earns a lot of money. She receives excellent benefits. She gets a long vacation each year. She works near her home. She has a good chance for promotion. Her boss likes her. Her secretary likes her. Ana wants to continue working for this company.

ACTIVITY C   *List each word or phrase in the paragraph that you don't understand. Then find the meaning and write it next to the word or phrase.*

_____   _____

_____   _____

_____   _____

ACTIVITY D   *Change the paragraph in Activity B.*

Imagine that Ana has a bad job. Begin your paragraph this way:

A Bad Job

Ana doesn't have a good job.

ACTIVITY E   *Think about a friend or relative who has a good job. Write the answers to the questions below and then tell your partner or group about a good job that a friend or relative has now.*

1. What kind of job does he/she have? *He/She* _____

2. How much does he/she earn? *He/She earns* _____

3. What are the benefits? *He/She has* _____

4. How much vacation time does he/she get. *He/She gets* _____

5. Is the job near his/her home? *The job is* _____

6. Does he/she like the other people? *He/She* _____

7. Does he/she want to continue working there? Why? *He/She* _____

ACTIVITY F   *Write a paragraph about a good job your friend or relative has.*

	[TITLE]
	My _____ has a good job. He/She

ACTIVITY G

Write your answers to the questions below and then tell your partner or your group about a bad job that someone you know has.

1. What kind of job does he/she have? _____

2. Does he/she earn much money? How much? _____

   He/She doesn't earn much money. He/She earns only _____

3. Does he/she get good benefits? Explain. _____

   _____

   _____

   _____

4. Does he/she get a good vacation? How much does he/she get?

   He/She doesn't get _____

   He/She only gets _____

5. Does he/she work near home? How does he/she get to work? How long does it take? _____

   _____

   _____

6. Does he/she have a chance for promotion? Explain. _____

   _____

   _____

7. Does he/she like the other people? Why or why not? _____

   _____

   _____

8. What does he/she want to do in the future? _____

   _____

   _____

ACTIVITY H   *Write a paragraph about the bad job described in Activity G.*

ADDITIONAL ACTIVITIES

1. Do paragraph 18 on page 139.

2. Write about a job you have now or had in the past. You may use the questions in Activity E or G to help you.

3. Write about something you do every day or every week. Tell what you like and don't like about it.

LESSON 10

A Favorite Sister

> *Study pages 124 and 160 before you do this lesson.*

ACTIVITY A *Work with your group or a partner.*

1. In the picture a brother and sister are dancing. List some of the things you and your favorite sister or brother or cousin like to do together.

   Example: <u>We like to dance.</u>

   a. _____

   b. _____

   c. _____

   d. _____

2. Here is a list of positive ways to describe people:

generous	kind	serious	neat
helpful	loving	talkative	studious
intelligent	affectionate	responsible	friendly
attractive	happy	hard-working	courteous (polite)

   Which of these qualities best describes your favorite sister or brother or cousin?

   _____ _____ _____ _____

   _____ _____ _____ _____

ACTIVITY B   *Read about Susan and Edward's favorite sister.*

A Favorite Sister

Susan and Edward have a favorite sister. They love her very much. They don't see her often because she lives in Alabama. Once in a while, they write to her or call her on the telephone. Next summer they will visit her when they take a vacation. They like to be with her because she is very affectionate with them.

ACTIVITY C   *List each word or phrase in the paragraph that you don't understand. Then find the meaning and write it next to the word or phrase.*

_____   _____

_____   _____

_____   _____

ACTIVITY D   *Change the paragraph in Activity B.*

Imagine that Susan and Edward have a favorite brother. Write about him. Begin this way:

A Favorite Brother

Susan and Edward have a favorite brother. They love him

ACTIVITY E   *Answer the questions.*

Example: What is the name of your favorite sister or brother or cousin?

My favorite sister's name is Maria.

1. Where does your favorite sister or brother or cousin live?

_____

2. What does he/she like to do?

_____

3. How often do you do things together?

_____

4. How much do you love him/her?

_____

5. How much does he/she love you?

_____

6. Why do you like to be together?

_____

ACTIVITY F   *Write sentences.*

Look at the positive qualities that you listed in Activity A. Select two of them. Use these words to write about your favorite sister or brother or cousin. Tell why he/she has the qualities that you selected.

Examples: _My favorite sister Maria is attractive. She has a_
beautiful face and long dark hair.

My favorite brother Daniel is neat. He keeps his
bedroom and his car very clean.

1. _____

_____

2. _____

_____

ACTIVITY G

Write about your favorite sister or brother or cousin. You may use some sentences from Activity E, Activity F, and the paragraph in Activity B. But also add some more of your own sentences. Include a title.

[TITLE]

ADDITIONAL ACTIVITIES

1. Do paragraph 20 on page 140.

2. If you don't live with your favorite sister or brother or cousin, write a letter to him or her. In the letter explain why he or she is your favorite.

LESSON 11

A Noisy Neighbor

Study pages 124, 125, and 160 before you do this lesson.

ACTIVITY A   *Work with your group or a partner.*

1. List some of the things that good neighbors do.

   Example: <u>They keep the neighborhood clean.</u>

   a. _____

   b. _____

2. Make a list of some of the things your neighbors do that you don't like.

   Example: <u>They make too much noise.</u>

   a. _____

   b. _____

3. Tell about the last time that you spoke to a neighbor. What did you talk about?

ACTIVITY B   *Read about a noisy neighbor.*

A Noisy Neighbor

My neighbor plays his radio too loudly. I talk to him in a nice way about the noise. I try to be reasonable with him, but the noise continues. Then I complain to him again and tell him that I am going to call the police. The noise stops, but only for a while. It is hard to live in peace with people like him.

ACTIVITY C   *List each word or phrase in the paragraph that you don't understand. Then find the meaning and write it next to the word or phrase.*

_____   _____

_____   _____

_____   _____

ACTIVITY D   *Change the paragraph in Activity B.*

Imagine that there are several noisy neighbors in your building or neighborhood. Write about these neighbors. Begin your paragraph this way:

Noisy Neighbors

My neighbors play their radios too loudly. I talk to them

ACTIVITY E   *Write a story.*

Write about a neighbor that you like or don't like and tell why you like or don't like this person.

[TITLE]

ACTIVITY F   *Write a dialogue.*

Imagine that you have a problem with one of your neighbors; for example, your neighbor makes too much noise or doesn't keep the area in front of his/her house or apartment clean. With a partner write the conversation that you would like to have with your neighbor in order to resolve the problem that you have with him/her. If you need more space, continue on your own paper.

	[TITLE]
	Me:
	Neighbor:

ADDITIONAL ACTIVITIES

1. Do paragraph 21 on page 141.

2. Write a letter to your landlord or to a city agency complaining about one of your neighbors.

LESSON 12

Summer Camp

> **Study page 163 before you do this lesson.**

ACTIVITY A   *Work with your group or a partner.*

1. Make a list of people who work with or take care of children.

   Example: camp counselors
   _____   _____   _____

   _____   _____   _____

2. Do you work with or take care of children now? If yes, tell what you do.

3. Do you plan to work with or take care of children in the future? What do you plan to do?

4. Make a list of activities that you do, or plan to do, with children.

   Example: I read books to them.

   I plan to teach them.

   a. _____

   b. _____

ACTIVITY B   *Read about Margaret and her husband Peter.*

Summer Camp

Every summer Margaret and her husband Peter work in a summer camp for deaf children. They spend two weeks of summer vacation at the camp. They live in a cabin with eight children. They speak sign language with the children. They play with the children during the day and put them to bed at night. Margaret and Peter enjoy the time they spend at the camp. They like the children a lot.

ACTIVITY C   *List each word or phrase in the paragraph that you don't understand. Then find the meaning and write it next to the word or phrase.*

_____   _____

_____   _____

_____   _____

ACTIVITY D   *Change the paragraph in Activity B.*

Now only Margaret works in the summer camp because Peter has a new job and works during the summer. Begin your paragraph this way:

Summer Camp

Every summer Margaret works

ACTIVITY E   *Complete each sentence.*

1. My friend _____ likes children because _____

_____

2. My friend works with children. In his/her job he/she _____

_____

3. My friend plays with children in his/her free time. He/She _____

_____

4. My friend thinks that children _____

_____

ACTIVITY F   *Write a paragraph.*

Write a paragraph about someone you know who works or plays with children. Tell what this person does and why he/she likes children. Be sure to include a title.

ACTIVITY G   *Write a paragraph.*

Write about a child that you know. Describe this child and tell about the things you do together. Also tell how you feel about this child. Be sure to include a title.

ADDITIONAL ACTIVITIES

1. Do paragraphs 14 and 15 on pages 137 and 138.

2. Read a storybook to a child. Then write about the following:
   Describe the child.
   What did you read?
   Did the child like the book? Why or why not?
   What did the child do and say while you were reading?
   Did you enjoy the experience?
   Do you plan to do it again?

LESSON 13

The Storekeeper

Study page 162 before you do this lesson.

ACTIVITY A   *Work with your group or a partner.*

1. What kind of store is this? _____

2. List some of the things they sell in this store.

_____   _____   _____

_____   _____   _____

_____   _____   _____

3. Write some of the reasons people like to shop in this store.

   Example: It stays open late.

   a. _____

   b. _____

   c. _____

4. List some words to describe the storekeeper.

   Example: friendly

_____   _____   _____

ACTIVITY B   *Read about a storekeeper.*

The Storekeeper

Everyone in the neighborhood shops at Kim's Grocery Store. Mr. Kim has a friendly smile for everyone. He keeps his store very clean. He sells good quality products at reasonable prices. He treats his customers well. He wants everyone to be satisfied.

ACTIVITY C   *List each word or phrase in the paragraph that you don't understand. Then find the meaning and write it next to the word or phrase.*

_____   _____

_____   _____

_____   _____

ACTIVITY D   *Change the paragraph in Activity B.*

Imagine that no one in the neighborhood likes to shop at Kim's grocery store. Write the paragraph again. Begin your paragraph this way:

The Storekeeper

No one in the neighborhood likes to shop at Kim's Grocery Store. Mr. Kim doesn't have a friendly smile

ACTIVITY E   *Think about a store in your neighborhood that you like. Then write your answers to the questions below and tell your partner or group about the store and the shopkeeper or store manager or clerk.*

1. What is the person's name? _____

2. What kind of store does he/she work in?_____

3. Where is the store located?_____

4. What kind of person is he/she?

   Example: _____ helpful _____

   _____ _____ _____ _____

5. Tell why you like this person. _____

   _____

   _____

6. Why do you shop there? _____

   _____

   _____

ACTIVITY F   *Write a paragraph about the person and the store in your neighborhood.*

_____

_____

_____

_____

_____

_____

_____

_____

ACTIVITY G   *Write sentences about a store you don't like to shop in and tell your partner or group about the store.*

1. Does the store open and close at convenient hours? _____

   The store doesn't open until _____ *and it closes at* _____.

2. Does the store charge fair prices? _____

   _____

3. Does the store sell the products you like? _____

   _____

4. Does it stock fresh food?_____

   _____

5. Does the storekeeper or manager or clerk try to be helpful? _____

   _____

6. Does he/she keep the place clean?_____

   _____

7. Does he/she remember your name? give you credit? cash your checks? accept food stamps? exchange bad items?

   _____

   _____

53

ACTIVITY H   *Write a paragraph about a store and a storekeeper, clerk, or manager you don't like.*

ADDITIONAL ACTIVITIES

1. Do paragraph 19 on page 140.

2. Write about a person you work with at a job or in school. Tell what you like and don't like about this person.

54

LESSON 14

A Strict Father

Study pages 125 and 161 before you do this lesson.

ACTIVITY A   *Work with your group or a partner.*

With their children parents can be:

strict   lenient   abusive   kind
unsympathetic   understanding   uncaring   caring

1. Which of these words best describes your mother?

_____ _____ _____ _____

2. Which of these words best describes your father?

_____ _____ _____ _____

3. Which of these words best describes you as a parent or the way you want to be as a parent when you have children?

_____ _____ _____ _____

ACTIVITY B   *Read about a strict father.*

A Strict Father

My friend Tom has five children. All of his children are teenage girls. They love to have fun. They like to dance and go to parties. My friend doesn't let his daughters go out. He says that they are too young. He doesn't want his daughters to get into trouble. Tom is very strict with his children.

ACTIVITY C   *List each word or phrase in the paragraph that you don't understand. Then find the meaning and write it next to the word or phrase.*

_____   _____

_____   _____

_____   _____

ACTIVITY D   *Change the paragraph in Activity B.*

Imagine that you know a strict mother named Mary who has five teenage daughters. Write about them. Begin your paragraph this way:

A Strict Mother

My friend Mary has five children. All of her children

ACTIVITY E   *Work with your group or a partner.*

Some parents don't want their teenage daughters to go out. What are the reasons?

Example: <u>They don't want them to get into trouble.</u>

1. *They don't want them to* _____

2. _____

3. _____

4. _____

5. _____

6. _____

7. _____

8. _____

ACTIVITY F   *Work with your group or a partner.*

Why does a teenage girl want her parents to let her go out?

Example: <u>She wants to have fun with her friends.</u>

1. _____

2. _____

3. _____

4. _____

5. _____

6. _____

7. _____

8. _____

ACTIVITY G   *Write a dialogue with your partner.*

Mary's daughters or Tom's daughters want to go to a party with their friends. The oldest daughter talks to her mother or father. Write the conversation. If you need more space, continue on your own paper.

[TITLE]

ADDITIONAL ACTIVITIES

1. Do paragraph 26 on page 143.

2. Write about a family that has teenage daughters. Tell what the daughters are permitted to do. Tell what the daughters are not permitted to do. Tell how the daughters feel about this.

LESSON 15

Maria's Apartment

> *Study pages 125 and 161 before you do this lesson.*

ACTIVITY A   *Work with your group or a partner.*

1. List some of the things that often need repair in a house or apartment.

   Example: _____ a faucet _____   _____ the refrigerator _____

   _____   _____   _____

   _____   _____   _____

2. Talk about your house or apartment. What do you want to change in order to make it a better place to live?

   Example: _____ I want to get a new refrigerator. _____

   _____

   _____

ACTIVITY B   *Read about Maria's apartment.*

Maria's Apartment

Maria lives in an apartment on Morris Avenue. Her apartment is small and dark. There are roaches and mice in her kitchen. The toilet in her bathroom is broken. The building is always dirty. Her neighbors make too much noise. Maria doesn't like her apartment. She doesn't like her neighbors, either. She wants to move to another neighborhood.

ACTIVITY C   *List each word or phrase in the paragraph that you don't understand. Then find the meaning and write it next to the word or phrase.*

_____   _____

_____   _____

_____   _____

ACTIVITY D   *Change the paragraph in Activity B.*

John has an apartment in the same building as Maria and he has similar problems. Write about John's apartment. Begin your paragraph this way:

John's Apartment

John lives in an apartment on Morris Avenue. His apartment

ACTIVITY E *Write a description.*

Write a description of your house or apartment. If you like your house or apartment, write about it in a positive way. If you don't like your house or apartment, write about it in a negative way.

ACTIVITY F   *Write a dialogue.*

Maria (or John) doesn't have a nice landlord. Maria (or John) talks to the landlord about the problems in the apartment. With a partner write the conversation that you and your partner imagine Maria (or John) is having with the landlord. If you need more space, continue on your own paper.

ADDITIONAL ACTIVITIES

1. Do paragraphs 24 and 25 on pages 142 and 143.

2. Write about your plans for the future. Do you plan to move to another house or apartment? Why or why not?

3. Write about your favorite room in your house or apartment. Describe this room and tell why it is your favorite.

LESSON 16

A Disabled Person

Study pages 124, 125, and 160 before you do this lesson.

ACTIVITY A   *Write the answers to the questions below and then discuss them with your partner or group.*

1. Why is the man in the wheelchair? Write some possible reasons.

   Example: ___He is paralyzed.___

   a. _____

   b. _____

2. Who is the person standing? List some possible answers.

   Example: ___A friend___

   _____   _____   _____

3. Why is the man in the wheelchair smiling?

   Example: ___He is smiling because he likes to be with his___
   ___friend.___

   a. _____

   b. _____

ACTIVITY B   *Read about the person standing in the picture. He is thinking about Stephen.*

A Disabled Person

Stephen is disabled. He has to use a wheelchair. I go to see him often. I like to be near him. I don't pity him. I am learning from him. He is happier than I am. He has more peace and love in him. I want to know why. I want to be like him.

ACTIVITY C   *List each word or phrase in the paragraph that you don't understand. Then find the meaning and write it next to the word or phrase.*

_____   _____

_____   _____

_____   _____

ACTIVITY D   *Change the paragraph in Activity B.*

Imagine that the person in the wheelchair is a woman named Barbara. The person standing in the picture is thinking about Barbara. Begin your paragraph this way:

A Disabled Person

Barbara is disabled. She has to use a wheelchair. I go to see her

ACTIVITY E

Complete the sentences below and then tell your partner or your group about a disabled person you know.

1. *The person's name is* _____

2. *His/Her problem is* _____

3. *I met him/her* _____

4. *I like/don't like him/her because* _____

5. *I see him/her* _____

6. *He/She makes me feel* _____ *because* _____

_____

ACTIVITY F

Write a paragraph about a disabled person.

ACTIVITY G   *Write a dialogue.*

With a partner, give a name to the person with Stephen in the photograph. This person wants to know why Stephen is happy even though he is disabled. Write a conversation between the two people. If you need more space, continue on your own paper.

_____

ADDITIONAL ACTIVITIES

1. Do paragraph 22 on page 141.

2. Write a letter to the mayor telling what your city should do to help disabled people. Tell why the government has a responsibility to help these people.

3. Some disabled people want to be called "physically challenged." Why do you think they prefer this term?

LESSON 17

My Neighborhood

Study pages 125 and 161 before you do this lesson.

ACTIVITY A   *Work with your group or a partner.*

Here is a list of vocabulary about neighborhoods. Which words and phrases describe your neighborhood?

nice houses	friendly neighbors	drug-free
nice buildings	unfriendly neighbors	too many drug addicts
old houses	quiet neighbors	alcohol-free
old buildings	noisy neighbors	too many alcoholics
dirty houses	clean streets	crime-free
dirty buildings	dirty streets	too much crime
many children	poor	good schools
only a few children	middle-class	inadequate schools
safe	a nice area for children	tree-lined streets
unsafe	a bad area for children	streets with no trees

_____   _____   _____

_____   _____   _____

_____   _____   _____

_____   _____   _____

ACTIVITY B   *Read about someone's opinion of his/her neighborhood.*

My Neighborhood

I don't like my neighborhood. There are many drug addicts on my block. Many people play loud music in front of my building. The street is always dirty. My children's school is not good. The neighborhood park is dangerous. The local supermarket is too expensive. My neighborhood is not a good place to raise my children.

ACTIVITY C   *List each word or phrase in the paragraph that you don't understand. Then find the meaning and write it next to the word or phrase.*

_____   _____

_____   _____

_____   _____

ACTIVITY D   *Change the paragraph in Activity B.*

Imagine that a husband and wife don't like the neighborhood where they are living. Write about them. Begin your paragraph this way:

Our Neighborhood

My husband and I don't like our neighborhood.

ACTIVITY E   *Work with your group or a partner.*

1. List some things you like about your neighborhood.

   Example: _My street is always clean._

   a. _____

   b. _____

   c. _____

   d. _____

   e. _____

   f. _____

   g. _____

   h. _____

2. List some things you don't like about your neighborhood.

   Example: _The buildings look old and dirty._

   a. _____

   b. _____

   c. _____

   d. _____

   e. _____

   f. _____

   g. _____

   h. _____

ACTIVITY F   *Write a description.*

Write about your neighborhood. Tell what you like and don't like about your neighborhood. Use some of the words, phrases and sentences that you wrote in Activity A and Activity E. You may also use some of the words and sentences from the paragraph in Activity B. Be sure to include a title. If you need more space, continue on your own paper.

ADDITIONAL ACTIVITIES

1. Do paragraph 23 on page 142.

2. Write a dialogue between a husband and wife. The husband likes the neighborhood and wants to stay there. The wife doesn't like the neighborhood and wants to move. Do this activity with a partner.

70

LESSON 18

Living Alone

> *Study pages 124 and 164 before you do this lesson.*

ACTIVITY A   *Work with your group or a partner.*

1. Which of the following words and phrases apply more to a married person or to a single person?

more responsibilities   more problems   more friends
children   more love   happier
more freedom   lonelier   more communication
more companionship   more housework

A married person   *A single person*

_____   _____

_____   _____

_____   _____

_____   _____

2. Choose one of the words or phrases you wrote. Explain why you put it in *A married person* column or *A single person* column.

3. In your opinion, is it better to be single or married? Why?

ACTIVITY B   *Read about a single person.*

Living Alone

I live by myself. I prefer it that way. I like my freedom. I cook for myself, and I clean the apartment. When I want company, I invite my friends to my apartment. When I need advice, I call my father. I enjoy the life of a single person.

ACTIVITY C   *List each word or phrase in the paragraph that you don't understand. Then find the meaning and write it next to the word or phrase.*

_____   _____

_____   _____

_____   _____

ACTIVITY D   *Change the paragraph in Activity B.*

The single person in Activity B got married a few months ago. Write about this person's life before he/she got married. Begin your paragraph this way:

Living Alone

Before I got married, I lived by myself.

ACTIVITY E   *Write sentences.*

1. Complete either A or B, but not both:

   a. *I like/don't like my life as a single person because* _____

   _____

   b. *I like/don't like my life as a married person because* _____

   _____

2. Complete both of the following sentences:

   a. *In general, single people* _____

   b. *In general, married people* _____

ACTIVITY F   *Write a paragraph.*

Describe your life now as a single person or as a married person.

ACTIVITY G   *Write a paragraph.*

Think of a person you know who is married. Describe this person's life before he/she got married. Or, describe your life before you were married.

ADDITIONAL ACTIVITIES

1. Do paragraphs 28 and 29 on pages 144 and 145.

2. Write a letter to someone who is planning to get married. Give this person some advice.

LESSON 19

The Interview

Study page 165 before you do this lesson.

ACTIVITY A   *Work with your group or a partner.*

1. The person in the picture was applying for a job. Write some questions the interviewer asked him.

   Example: _Do you have a high school diploma?_

   a. _____

   b. _____

   c. _____

   d. _____

2. Answer the following questions:

   a. How did the person in the picture prepare for the interview?
   b. What did he do to make a good impression?
   c. Did he get what he wanted?
   d. How did he feel after the interview?

ACTIVITY B   *Read about a job interview.*

The Job Interview

John arrived on time for his job interview. He felt relaxed. He filled out the application form correctly. He spoke with the personnel director confidently. John impressed her with his qualifications. The interview went very well. The personnel director called him a few days later. John got the job.

ACTIVITY C   *List each word or phrase in the paragraph that you don't understand. Then find the meaning and write it next to the word or phrase.*

_____   _____

_____   _____

_____   _____

ACTIVITY D   *Change the paragraph in Activity B.*

Imagine that John did not have a good interview. Change everything to the negative. Begin your paragraph this way.

The Job Interview

John didn't arrive on time for his job interview.

ACTIVITY E   *Work with your group or a partner.*

Answer the following questions about an interview you had in the past. For example, tell about an interview you had by a doctor or nurse, government or school official, or an employer.

1. What was the interview for?

2. Where did you go for the interview?

3. Whom did you talk to?

4. How did you dress?

5. Write some questions that they asked you.

_____

_____

_____

_____

6. How did you feel after the interview?

7. Did you get what you wanted? Explain.

ACTIVITY F   *Write a paragraph about the interview.*

ACTIVITY F   *Write a story about Pedro Cabrera.*

He went for a job interview, but he didn't get the job. What did he do wrong? Did he dress properly? Did he arrive on time? Did he speak in English? Did he speak correctly? Explain. Did he feel good after the interview? If you need more space, continue on your own paper.

ADDITIONAL ACTIVITIES

1. Do paragraphs 30 and 31 on pages 145 and 146.

2. Interview a partner. Ask the following questions:

   a. What is your name? b. Where do you live? c. Where were you born? d. What is your phone number? e. When did you arrive in the United States? f. Why did you come to the United States? g. Why did you enroll in this school?

3. Write a brief composition about your partner.

LESSON 20

A Close Friend

Study pages 124 and 166 before you do this lesson.

ACTIVITY A   *Work with your group or a partner.*

1. Write some of the things that close friends like to do together.

    Example: _They like to go to the movies._
    They like to shop.

    a. _____

    b. _____

    c. _____

    d. _____

    e. _____

79

2. The two friends in the picture on page 79 are similar in some ways.

   Example: _They are both athletic._

   Write some of the ways you and a close friend are similar.

   Example: _Both of us are intelligent._
   We are both students.

   a. _____

   b. _____

   c. _____

   d. _____

   e. _____

   f. _____

   g. _____

3. The two friends in the picture on page 79 are different in some ways.

   Example: _One likes to read but the other doesn't._

   Write some of the ways you and a close friend are different.

   Example: _I like to jog but my friend doesn't._

   a. _____

   b. _____

   c. _____

   d. _____

   e. _____

   f. _____

   g. _____

ACTIVITY B   *Read about two friends.*

A Close Friend

My friend and I are always together. We are the same age. We are interested in the same things. We are in the same class in school. Both of us are intelligent. Both of us are popular with our classmates. In many ways we are alike.

ACTIVITY C   *List each word or phrase in the paragraph that you don't understand. Then find the meaning and write it next to the word or phrase.*

_____   _____

_____   _____

_____   _____

ACTIVITY D   *Change the paragraph in Activity B.*

Write about a friend you had in the past. Begin your paragraph this way:

A Close Friend

Before my friend moved to France, he and I were

ACTIVITY E   *Work with your group or a partner.*

Answer the following questions about a friend in the United States.

1. What is your friend's name?
2. Where is he/she from?
3. How old is he/she?
4. Where does he/she live?
5. What do you do together?
6. In what ways are you alike?
7. In what ways are you different?
8. Why is he/she a close friend?

ACTIVITY F   *Write a paragraph about your friend.*

ACTIVITY G   *Work with your group or a partner.*

Answer the following questions about a friend you had in your native country.

1. What was your friend's name?

2. Where was he/she born?

3. Where did he/she live?

4. What did you do together?

5. In what ways were you alike?

6. In what ways were you different?

7. Why was he/she a close friend?

ACTIVITY H   *Write a paragraph about a close friend you had in your native country.*

ADDITIONAL ACTIVITIES

1. Do paragraphs 32, 33, and 34 on pages 146 and 147.

2. Write a letter to your friend in your native country. Tell him/her about your friend here. Tell how the two friends are alike. Tell how the two friends are different. Tell if they would like each other. Why?

LESSON 21

Speaking With . . .

Study pages 125 and 167 before you do this lesson.

ACTIVITY A   *In the picture a father is talking to his son. With your partner or group, write some of the things they could be speaking about.*

Example: The son failed a class in school.

1. _____

2. _____

3. _____

ACTIVITY B   *The young person in the picture on page 84 is talking to his father. Here is what he says:*

Speaking with Father

Every morning when I wake up, I say "Good Morning" to my father. I have a conversation with him. I feel very comfortable with him. I speak to him about my life, my problems, and my desires. I tell him everything. I spend about 15 minutes with him. Then I get ready for school.

ACTIVITY C   *List each word or phrase in the paragraph that you don't understand. Then find the meaning and write it next to the word or phrase.*

_____   _____

_____   _____

_____   _____

ACTIVITY D   *Change the paragraph in Activity B.*

The young person is telling about what happened yesterday. Change *Every morning* to *Yesterday morning* and write the paragraph in the past tense. Begin your paragraph this way:

Speaking with Father

Yesterday morning when I woke up,

ACTIVITY E   *Work with your group or a partner.*

1. Who is the person you talk to most about your problems and desires? _____

_____

2. When did you last speak to that person?_____

3. Tell some of the things you spoke about.

Example: _*We spoke about my problems in school.*_

_____

_____

_____

4. Did the conversation help you solve any problems or answer any questions? Explain.

ACTIVITY F   *Write a paragraph about a conversation you had with someone. Tell whom you spoke to, when you had the conversation, and what you spoke about.*

ACTIVITY G   *Write a dialogue.*

You had a problem and you talked to a friend or relative about it. Write the conversation you had. If you need more space, continue on your own paper.

ADDITIONAL ACTIVITIES

1. Do paragraphs 35 and 36 on page 148.

2. Write about a problem you had in your native country. Tell what you did about it. Did anyone help you?

LESSON 22

Communicating

Study pages 125 and 168 before you do this lesson.

ACTIVITY A   *The young man in the picture has trouble communicating because he can't speak English very well. Write some things he can do to improve his speaking ability.*

Example: *He can watch English language programs on television.*

1. _____

2. _____

3. _____

4. _____

ACTIVITY B *Read about Francisco.*

Communicating

Francisco can't communicate in English. He can't speak the language. He can't read it. He can't write it. He can understand only a few words. Francisco can't relax when he is with English-speaking people. He can't act like a normal person because he can't carry on a conversation.

ACTIVITY C *List each word or phrase in the paragraph that you don't understand. Then find the meaning and write it next to the word or phrase.*

_____   _____

_____   _____

_____   _____

ACTIVITY D *Change the paragraph in Activity B.*

Francisco can communicate better now. Write about his problem in the past. Begin your paragraph this way:

Communicating

When Francisco first came to the United States, he couldn't communicate

ACTIVITY E   *Work with your group or a partner.*

Tell about the things you couldn't do when you first came to the United States because you didn't know much English.

Example: *I couldn't ask for directions.*

1. *I couldn't* _____

2. _____

3. _____

4. _____

5. _____

ACTIVITY F   *Tell a story about an experience you had in the past trying to speak English.*

ACTIVITY G   *Tell your partner or your group about the things you can do now that you couldn't do before because your English is better.*

Example: *I can understand the people on television.*

1. _____

2. _____

3. _____

4. _____

5. _____

ACTIVITY H   *Write about a good experience you had speaking to someone in English.*

ADDITIONAL ACTIVITIES

1. Do paragraph 37 on page 149.

2. Write about the things you do to improve your English.

3. With your partner, write a dialogue. Pretend you are two people meeting for the first time at a party.

LESSON 23

A Serious Conversation

Study pages 124, 125, and 160 before you do this lesson.

ACTIVITY A *Work with your group or a partner.*

1. What are some serious things that you talk about with a friend or relative?

   Example: <u>*I talk about my family.*</u>

   a. _____

   b. _____

   c. _____

2. When was the last time you had a serious conversation with someone? _____

3. What was the conversation about? _____

92

ACTIVITY B   *Read about Richard and Maria's conversation.*

Maria is a young woman who came to the United States alone. In the following paragraph Maria is telling us about her conversation with her boyfriend, Richard.

A Serious Conversation

Last night I had a serious conversation with Richard. I talked to him about many things. I showed him a letter from my mother. I told him that I had to go back to my country. I told him that I loved him but that I was not ready to marry him now. He felt very sad.

ACTIVITY C   *List each word or phrase in the paragraph that you don't understand. Then find the meaning and write it next to the word or phrase.*

_____   _____

_____   _____

_____   _____

ACTIVITY D   *Change the paragraph in Activity B.*

Imagine that John is a young man who came to the United States alone. He had a conversation with his girlfriend, Jennifer. John tells us about his conversation with Jennifer. Begin your paragraph this way:

A Serious Conversation

Last night I had a serious conversation with Jennifer. I talked to her about many things.

ACTIVITY E   *Write a dialogue.*

Recently you had a serious conversation with someone. You talked about a problem. Write the conversation you had. If you need more space, continue on your own paper.

ACTIVITY F   *Finish the letter.*

In Activity D you wrote a paragraph about John. Below is the beginning of the letter that John's mother wrote to him. Work with a partner and together finish the letter.

December 14,

Dear John,
    I hope that you are fine and that everything is going well with you. I am sorry that I have to write to you at this time, but I have some very bad news to tell you.

ADDITIONAL ACTIVITIES

1. Do paragraph 27 on page 144.

2. Write a letter to someone you know. Write a happy letter, a sad letter, or an angry letter.

3. With a partner write a story about what happened to John after he went back to his country. What did he do when he arrived there? Did he feel happy or sad? Why? Did he continue to love Jennifer or did he forget about her? Did he stay there or did he come back to the United States?

LESSON 24

The Future

> **Study page 169 before you do this lesson.**

ACTIVITY A   *Work with your group or a partner.*

The young man and woman in the picture are graduating from school. They are thinking about their future. When you think about your future, what do you think you will do?

Example: ___Maybe I will continue my education.___

1. *Perhaps I will get a job as a* _____

2. _____

3. _____

4. _____

ACTIVITY B   *Read the young man's thoughts about the future.*

My Future

I have to think about the future. I will graduate from high school next year. I don't know what I will do after I graduate. Maybe I will go to college. Maybe I will get married. I need to talk to a counselor because I need some advice.

ACTIVITY C   *List each word or phrase in the paragraph that you don't understand. Then find the meaning and write it next to the word or phrase.*

_____   _____

_____   _____

_____   _____

ACTIVITY D   *Change the paragraph in Activity B.*

The young man and young woman, Freddy and Lisa, are both graduating and both thinking about the future. Tell about both Freddy and Lisa. Begin your paragraph this way:

Freddy and Lisa's Future

Freddy and Lisa need to think about the future. They will

ACTIVITY E   *Work with your group or a partner.*

Tell what you will do when you finish this school. Use the sentences below to help you.

1. *When I finish school I will* _____

2. *I will also* _____

3. *Maybe I will* _____

4. *I would like to* _____

5. *I also want to* _____

ACTIVITY F   *Write a paragraph about your plans for the future. Begin your paragraph this way:*

My Future

When I finish school I will

ACTIVITY G   *Write about your partner or some people in your group. Tell what they will do when they finish this school.*

ADDITIONAL ACTIVITIES

1. Do paragraph 4 on page 132.

2. Imagine you can do anything you want to in the future. Write about what you will do.

LESSON 25

Holiday

Study pages 124 and 169 before you do this lesson.

ACTIVITY A   *Work with your group or a partner.*

1. The man and woman in the picture are decorating a Christmas tree. Make a list of some of the ornaments or decorations that people use during Christmas.

   Example: _____ *lights* _____

   _____ _____ _____

   _____ _____ _____

2. Write the names of the holidays you celebrate during the year.

   _____ _____

   _____ _____

   _____ _____

ACTIVITY B   *Read a husband's description of Christmas Eve.*

Christmas Eve

Every Christmas my wife and I play Santa Claus for our children. On Christmas Eve we put up the Christmas tree in the living room. We decorate the tree with lights. Next we wrap the presents and put them under the tree. My wife and I enjoy doing this for our children. We finish about one o'clock in the morning. Then we go to bed, tired but happy.

ACTIVITY C   *List each word or phrase in the paragraph that you don't understand. Then find the meaning and write it next to the word or phrase.*

_____   _____

_____   _____

_____   _____

ACTIVITY D   *Change the paragraph in Activity B.*

The man telling the story about Christmas Eve wants to talk about next Christmas. Begin your paragraph this way:

Next Christmas

Next Christmas my wife and I will

101

ACTIVITY E

Complete the sentences below and then tell the people in your group about your favorite holiday. Tell them how you will celebrate it next time.

1. *My favorite holiday is* _____

2. *I like it because* _____

3. *On this holiday I usually* _____

4. *Next time I will* _____

5. *I probably will not (won't)* _____

6. *I would like to* _____

7. *I also want to* _____

ACTIVITY F

Write two paragraphs about your favorite holiday.

In the first paragraph, tell how you and your family usually celebrate the holiday. In the second paragraph, tell how you *will/would like to/want to* celebrate the holiday next time. Write about some things you *won't* do. If you need more space, continue on your own paper.

ACTIVITY G   *Write a story.*

Describe the best holiday celebration that you remember. Tell when you celebrated this holiday, what happened, and why it was the best you can remember.

ADDITIONAL ACTIVITIES

1. Do paragraph 38 on page 149.

2. Write a letter. Invite a friend or relative to your home to celebrate a holiday. Tell him/her what you will do together.

LESSON 26

Learning To Be Responsible

Study pages 125 and 169 before you do this lesson.

ACTIVITY A   *Work with your group or a partner.*

1. Make a list of household chores that pre-teenage children can learn to do and be responsible for.

   Example: *wash the dishes*

   _____   _____

   _____   _____

2. Which household chores were you responsible for when you were a child?

   Example: *I had to take out the garbage.*

   a. _____

   b. _____

   c. _____

ACTIVITY B   *Read about a young girl and boy who are learning to be responsible.*

Learning to Be Responsible

My daughter Kim and my son Mike are learning to be responsible. Each morning they make their beds and clean their rooms. They iron their own clothes for school. Each afternoon they set the table for dinner. After dinner they wash the dishes and take out the garbage. On Saturdays they help me with the laundry. They also help me to clean the house. I am proud of my children.

ACTIVITY C   *List each word or phrase in the paragraph that you don't understand. Then find the meaning and write it next to the word or phrase.*

_____   _____

_____   _____

_____   _____

ACTIVITY D   *Change the paragraph in Activity B.*

Imagine that Kim and Mike are only four and five years old. They are too young to help with the housework. They will learn to be responsible for household chores when they are nine and ten years old. Write about Kim and Mike when they are nine and ten years old. Begin your paragraph this way:

Learning to Be Responsible

When Kim and Mike are nine and ten years old, they will learn to be responsible. Each morning

105

ACTIVITY E   *Write sentences.*

Write sentences about the things you need to be more responsible for.

Example: *I need to be more responsible for doing my homework because it will help me learn English.*

1. _____

   _____

2. _____

   _____

3. _____

   _____

ACTIVITY F   *Write a paragraph.*

Write about some specific things that you will do to become more responsible.

ACTIVITY G   *Write a story.*

Write about a child or children you know who do some of the housework in their home.

ADDITIONAL ACTIVITIES

1. Do paragraph 39 on page 150.

2. Write a dialogue with a partner. Write a dialogue between a parent and child who does not want to help with the housework.

LESSON 27

Autumn

Study pages 124 and 170 before you do this lesson.

ACTIVITY A   *Work with your group or a partner.*

1. List some of the things you like about the autumn season.

    Example: _I like the falling leaves._

    a. _____

    b. _____

    c. _____

2. List of some of the things you don't like about autumn.

    Example: _It's too cold for swimming._

    a. _____

    b. _____

    c. _____

ACTIVITY B   *Read about autumn.*

Autumn

Soon the days will grow shorter. The nights will grow colder. The beaches and the swimming pools will close. Children will return to school. The leaves on the trees will turn bright orange and red and yellow. Then they will fall to the ground. The birds will begin to fly south. We will go outside less often. We will stay inside in our warm houses.

ACTIVITY C   *List each word or phrase in the paragraph that you don't understand. Then find the meaning and write it next to the word or phrase.*

_____   _____

_____   _____

_____   _____

ACTIVITY D   *Change the paragraph in Activity B.*

Imagine that you are the author of the paragraph in Activity B and you want to rewrite the paragraph because you prefer to use the *going to* form. Begin your paragraph this way:

Autumn

Soon the days are going to grow shorter.

ACTIVITY E   *List some of the things you like to do during the other three seasons of the year.*

Summer	*Winter*	*Spring*
go swimming	*buy gifts*	*plant flowers*

ACTIVITY F   *Write a letter.*

Write a letter to a relative or friend and tell him/her what you are going to do in your favorite season.

ACTIVITY G   *Write a description.*

Describe your favorite season of the year. Tell why you like it. Write about some of the things you like to do during this season.

_____

ADDITIONAL ACTIVITIES

1. Do paragraphs 42 and 43 on pages 151 and 152.

2. Write a story about something you did last year during your favorite season.

3. Find two or three pictures showing scenes of your favorite season. Under each picture write a short paragraph explaining why you selected the picture.

LESSON 28

An Enjoyable Evening

> **Study pages 124, 125, and 170 before you do this lesson.**

ACTIVITY A   *Work with your group or a partner.*

1. The man and woman in the picture appear to be having a romantic dinner together. Make a list of some reasons why people have romantic dinners.

   Example: ____ *to celebrate a birthday* ____

   _____   _____

   _____   _____

   _____   _____

2. Imagine that you will cook dinner for someone special this evening. What will you cook and why?

3. Write things that you do to make an evening romantic.

   Example: ____ *I wear nice clothes.* _____

   _____

   _____

   _____

   _____

ACTIVITY B   *Read about a romantic evening.*

Someone promises to cook a friend's favorite dishes.

An Enjoyable Evening

I will cook for you tonight. I will make your favorite dishes. I will buy a nice bottle of wine. We will eat by candlelight. You will like the dinner. You will enjoy the whole evening.

ACTIVITY C   *List each word or phrase in the paragraph that you don't understand. Then find the meaning and write it next to the word or phrase.*

_____   _____

_____   _____

_____   _____

ACTIVITY D   *Change the paragraph in Activity B.*

Imagine you are the person speaking in the paragraph in Activity B. You usually speak about the future with the *going to* form, not the *will* form. Begin your paragraph this way:

An Enjoyable Evening

I am going to cook for you tonight.

ACTIVITY E   *Complete the sentences.*

1. *I would like to have a romantic evening with* _____

2. *My favorite place for a romantic dinner is* _____

3. *After a romantic dinner, I like* _____

ACTIVITY F   *Write two paragraphs.*

Write about a romantic evening that you plan to have. In the first paragraph tell about who you are going to spend this romantic evening with and when. In the second paragraph tell what you are going to do. If you need more space, continue on your own paper.

ACTIVITY G   *Write a dialogue.*

With a partner give names to the man and woman in the picture on page 112. Then write the conversation that you and your partner think the man and woman are having while they are eating. If you need more space, continue on your own paper.

ADDITIONAL ACTIVITIES

1. Do paragraphs 40 and 41 on pages 150 and 151.

2. Write a description of the person you would most like to spend a romantic evening with. Describe the positive qualities that this person has that make you want to be with him or her.

LESSON 29

The Cafeteria

Study pages 124 and 171 before you do this lesson.

ACTIVITY A   *Work with your group or a partner. List the activities happening in the picture.*

Example: *A few students are having a conversation.*

1. _____

2. _____

3. _____

4. _____

5. _____

6. _____

ACTIVITY B   *Read about a cafeteria.*

The Cafeteria

Every day many strange things happen in our cafeteria. A few students sleep on top of the tables. Many students copy their classmates' homework. Some boys and girls dance in the middle of the floor. A couple of boys throw food out the window. Several students smoke cigarettes in a corner. Some mice eat the garbage on the floor. What a mess!

ACTIVITY C   *List each word or phrase in the paragraph that you don't understand. Then find the meaning and write it next to the word or phrase.*

_____   _____

_____   _____

_____   _____

ACTIVITY D   *Change the paragraph in Activity B.*

The paragraph in Activity B tells what *usually* happens in the cafeteria. Change it to tell what is happening *right now*. Begin your paragraph this way:

The Cafeteria

Right now many strange things are happening

ACTIVITY E   *Work with your group or a partner.*

Tell what is happening right now in the classroom.

ACTIVITY F   *Write a paragraph.*

Describe what is happening in the classroom.

ACTIVITY G   *Work with a partner.*

1. Tell your partner about yourself and your family.
   a. Where are you living now? b. Whom are you living with? c. What are you doing now? d. Tell about your family.

2. Write your partner's answers below.

a. _____ *is living* _____
   (partner's name)

b. *He/She is living with* _____

c. *He/She is* _____

d. *His/Her family* _____

118

ACTIVITY H   *Write two paragraphs about your partner.*

In the first paragraph, use answers from Activity F on the previous page. In the second paragraph, write more about your partner. If you need more space, continue on your own paper.

ADDITIONAL ACTIVITIES

1. Do paragraph 44 on page 152.

2. Write a letter to someone in your native country telling what you are doing now.

LESSON 30

A Better Future

Study pages 125 and 171 before you do this lesson.

ACTIVITY A   *The young woman in the picture is thinking about her future. Write about the things you want for a better future.*

Example: *I want a good job.*

1. _____

2. _____

3. _____

4. _____

120

ACTIVITY B   *Read about Patricia's plans.*

A Better Future

Patricia lives with her aunt and uncle. She works part-time as a messenger. She earns only a few dollars per week. However, Patricia plans to go to college. She hopes to be an engineer. She plans to find a good job after graduation. Patricia looks forward to a better future for herself.

ACTIVITY C   *List each word or phrase in the paragraph that you don't understand. Then find the meaning and write it next to the word or phrase.*

_____   _____

_____   _____

_____   _____

ACTIVITY D   *Change the paragraph in Activity B.*

Change the first sentence of the paragraph to *Right now Patricia is living with her aunt and uncle,* and continue writing in the *present continuous tense.*

A Better Future

Right now Patricia is living with her aunt and uncle.

ACTIVITY E   *Tell about your best friend.*

Talk to the people in your group. Tell about your best friend.

1. What is his/her name?
2. Where is he/she living?
3. Whom is he/she living with?
4. What is he/she doing now?
5. What is he/she planning to do?
6. What is he/she hoping to become?
7. What is he/she looking forward to?
8. Tell one interesting thing about your friend.

ACTIVITY F   *Write two paragraphs about your best friend. If you need more space, continue on your own paper.*

ACTIVITY G   *Write a dialogue in which two people are discussing their plans for the future. If you need more space, continue on your own paper.*

ADDITIONAL ACTIVITIES

1. Do paragraph 45 on page 153.

2. Write about what you are doing now to make a better future for yourself.

A Model Letter

December 2, 1994

Dear Maria,

I hope that you and all your family are fine. I am writing to you because Freddy told me that you are coming to the United States soon. That is wonderful news! I am very happy for you. Everybody here is very excited. We can't wait to see you again. When you get here, we will have a big party for you.

Please write to me and let me know exactly when you are coming. Remember to bring a winter coat because the weather is very cold here.

Love,
Rosie

A Model Dialogue

<u>Complaining to a Neighbor</u>

Me: I need to talk to you.

Neighbor: What's the problem?

Me: It's the same problem as always. Your children are playing their radio too loudly.

Neighbor: O.K. I will tell them to lower the volume.

Me: This is the third time that I am talking to you about this. Why don't you control your children?

Neighbor: Listen, don't get nasty! I said I will talk to my children.

Me: I hope so. I need to have peace and quiet so that I can sleep.

Neighbor: Don't worry about it.

Me: This is the last time I'm going to complain to you about the noise. Next time I'm going to call the landlord.

SECTION TWO

Supplementary Paragraphs

Name _____ Class _____ Date_____

Checksheet for Supplementary Paragraphs

Paragraph	Date	Proof-read	Instructor		Paragraph	Date	Proof-read	Instructor
Ex	9/17	✔	DD		23			
1					24			
2					25			
3					26			
4					27			
5					28			
6					29			
7					30			
8					31			
9					32			
10					33			
11					34			
12					35			
13					36			
14					37			
15					38			
16					39			
17					40			
18					41			
19					41			
20					43			
21					44			
22					45			

Instructions: When you finish writing a paragraph, read it carefully to be sure there are no errors. You may also ask a partner to proofread it. When you think the paragraph is correct, write the date and put a check mark (✔) under "Proofread." Then your instructor or tutor will read the paragraph. If there are any errors, you must write the paragraph again. When it is correct, the instructor or tutor will write her/his initials.

1

The Surgeon

Clara is a surgeon. She works at Lincoln Hospital. She has to work many hours every week. She doesn't mind because she loves the medical profession. She really cares about people and wants to make them well. She is an excellent doctor.

Change ____Clara____ to ____David____. Begin the paragraph this way:

____David is a surgeon. He works . . .____

WRITING ACTIVITY   Tell about a job you want in the future. Tell why you want this job.

2

The Bank Executive

Mr. Reynoso works at the Chemical Bank. He is head of the student loan department. He is responsible for a lot of money each year. He checks every loan application carefully. He has to make sure that the students who apply really need the money. He enjoys this kind of work. He likes the responsibility.

Change ____Mr. Reynoso____ to ____Ms. Diaz____. Begin the paragraph this way:

____Ms. Diaz works at the Chemical Bank. She is . . .____

WRITING ACTIVITY   Tell about someone who works at your school who helped you with a financial problem or a study problem. Do you think this person likes his/her job?

3

A Lucky Woman?

I am a young woman. I am very happy because I am in love with a handsome, middle-aged man. I am crazy about him. I am planning to marry him. I am a very lucky person because I am sure of his love.

> Write about your friend, Susan. Begin the paragraph this way:
> Susan is a young woman. She is . . .

WRITING ACTIVITY   Is she a lucky person? Explain. Tell about someone you know who married a much younger or older person. Are they (Were they) happy? Explain.

4

Living Near the Airport

I am getting old. I live near the airport. I hear the planes all day and all night. The planes pass directly over the house. I get very nervous when a plane passes overhead. I don't like the noise. I don't like the danger. I want to move to a safer neighborhood. I need peace and quiet.

> Change ___I___ to ___Mr. & Mrs. Hutton___. Begin the paragraph this way:
> Mr. & Mrs. Hutton are getting old. They live . . .

WRITING ACTIVITY   Is your neighborhood a good place for older people to live? Is it safe and quiet? Is there convenient transportation? Are neighbors helpful?

5

My Class

My class is never the same. It is different each day. Sometimes it is interesting. Sometimes it is boring. Sometimes it is easy. Sometimes it is difficult. My class is like my life.

Change the title to _My Classes_ . Begin the paragraph this way:
My classes are never the same. They are . . .

WRITING ACTIVITY   Describe one of your classes. Is it interesting sometimes? Why? Is it boring sometimes? Explain.

6

My Father

My father is retired. He is old and sick. He is in a nursing home. He is too sick to live at home. My father is not happy in the nursing home. He is not comfortable there. He would like to come back home.

Change the title to _My Parents_ . Begin the paragraph this way:
My parents are retired. They are . . .

WRITING ACTIVITY   Tell about someone you know in a nursing home. Is that person happy? Explain. Is it better for an old and sick person to live at home or in a nursing home? Explain.

7

Don't Be Afraid

I am coming to see you. I need to talk to you. I want to tell you what a beautiful person you are. I want to tell you how much I love you. I want you to know how much we all love you. You don't have to be afraid. I will stay with you.

Change __I__ to __We__. Begin the paragraph this way:

We are coming to see you.

WRITING ACTIVITY   Write a letter to a friend who has a problem. Explain how you can help him/her.

8

The Right Person?

Mr. Goodman is qualified for the job. He is intelligent. He is well-educated. He is confident of his ability. He is interested in working for our company. He is ready to begin next week.

Change the paragraph to the negative. Begin the paragraph this way:

Mr. Goodman is not qualified for the job.

WRITING ACTIVITY   This paragraph gives five reasons why Mr. Goodman is qualified for a job. Write the reasons. Mr. Goodman is "intelligent" and "well educated." Are these different qualities? Explain.

134

9

Who is the Boss?

You are the head of this company. You are the chief who gives the orders. You are in charge of everything. You are the person who makes all the decisions. You are the one who pays the salaries and gives promotions. You are the boss.

Change the paragraph to the negative. Begin the paragraph this way:

You are not the head of this company.

WRITING ACTIVITY Tell about someone you work (worked) for. Do (Did) you like to work for this person? Explain.

10

A Great Place to Live?

This city is a great place to live. The air is clean and the streets are quiet. The transportation system is efficient. Food and rent are cheap. It is easy to find a job. People are friendly and helpful. It is safe to go out at night.

Change the paragraph to the negative. Begin the paragraph this way:

This city is not a great place to live.

WRITING ACTIVITY Tell how your city is the same as, or different from, the city in the paragraph.

11

Injustice

Juan and Carlos work on a plantation. They cut sugar cane. They have to work seven days a week. They stay in the hot sun all day long. Juan and Carlos get very little money. They eat and sleep in a shack. They live a terrible existence. They deserve more money and better working conditions.

Change __Juan and Carlos__ to __Pedro__. Begin the paragraph this way:
__Pedro works on a plantation.__

WRITING ACTIVITY   Tell about a person in this country or in your native country who works very hard and earns very little money. How can people like Juan and Carlos help themselves? How can other people help them?

12

Wonderful Parents

My parents are wonderful. They know that my life is very difficult right now. They help me in many ways. They give me advice. They take care of my children in an emergency. They comfort me when I am feeling depressed. My parents really love me. They make my life easier to live.

Change the title to __A Wonderful Mother__. Begin the paragraph this way:
__My mother is wonderful. She knows . . .__

WRITING ACTIVITY   Tell how your parents help you now or helped you in the past.

13

Ice Skating

Every winter my brother and I go ice skating. After school we run home and put on warm clothes. We take our ice skates and walk to the lake on the other side of town. We skate for a couple of hours until it gets dark. Then we build a fire to keep warm. At about 7:30 we return home because we know dinner is ready.

Change __My brother and I__ to __My brother__. Begin the paragraph this way:
__Every winter my brother goes ice . . .__

WRITING ACTIVITY Tell about something you do (did) for fun in your neighborhood or town.

14

A Second Home

Every summer I go to the Dominican Republic. I stay for one month. First I visit friends. Then I travel around the island. I see new places and I meet new people. Before I return to Chicago, I spend a week at Sosua Beach. I love the country and its people. When I go there, I feel like I have a second home.

Change __I__ to __Patricia__. Begin the paragraph this way:
__Every summer Patricia goes to the Dominican Republic.__

WRITING ACTIVITY Tell about someone who wants to go back to her/his native country. Explain the reasons.

15

The Writer

I write books for ESL students. I write because I enjoy it. I also write because I like students. I have fun creating new writing activities for students. When I finish a book, I send it to a publisher. If the publisher likes the book, I sign a contract. If not, I try again.

Change __I__ to _Professor Smith_ . Begin the paragraph this way:
Professor Smith writes books for ESL students. He writes because he . . .

WRITING ACTIVITY   Is it more important to work at a job you enjoy or a job that pays a lot of money? Give reasons.

16

History Class

We enjoy our history class. We like our teacher and classmates. We understand the history book. We take good notes in class. We do all the assignments. We study every night. We prepare well for the exams. We pass the exams with good grades. We feel satisfied with our work.

Make the paragraph negative. Begin the paragraph this way:
We don't enjoy our history class.

WRITING ACTIVITY   Which class or subject is your best? Tell why.

17

The Date

I have a good time when I am with you. I enjoy your company. I like your personality. I trust you. I feel secure with you. You make me feel special. You make me happy to be alive. I want to get to know you better. I want to see you again.

Change the paragraph to the negative. Begin the paragraph this way:
I don't have a good time when I am . . .

WRITING ACTIVITY   Tell about someone you met recently. Tell what you like and don't like about this person.

18

The Dog

The dog barks all night long. It keeps the neighbors awake. It chases cars. It scares the children. It bites the mailman. It fights with the cat all the time. The dog eats too much and it has fleas.

Change the paragraph to the negative. Begin the paragraph this way:
The dog doesn't bark all night long.

WRITING ACTIVITY   Tell about the advantages and disadvantages of having a dog in the city.

19

My Daughter's Boyfriend

My daughter's boyfriend impresses me. He dresses well. He appears neat and clean. He has good manners. He speaks politely. He knows how to carry on a conversation. He comes on time for a date, and he brings my daughter flowers. This young man is welcome in my house.

Change the paragraph to the negative. Begin the paragraph this way:

My daughter's boyfriend doesn't impress me.

WRITING ACTIVITY   Which of the following is the most important in a "boyfriend"? Which is the most important in a "girlfriend"? Explain your choices.

He/She dresses well.   He/She is generous.
He/She is neat and clean.   He/She is good-looking.
He/She has good manners.   He/She is intelligent.

20

My Love

Marilyn is my love. I think about her constantly. I call her every night to talk to her. When I see her, I feel full of love for her. I dream about her when I can't see her. I love her so much. I want to be with her forever.

Change ___Marilyn___ to ___Paul___. Begin the paragraph this way:

Paul is my love. I think about him . . .

WRITING ACTIVITY   Tell about someone you loved in the past. How did you show your love?

21

The Sponsor

Porn is a refugee from Thailand. I am responsible for her. I am helping her to get accustomed to life in the United States. I send her to school to learn English. When I think that she is lonely and homesick, I talk to her. I want her to be happy in this strange country.

Change __Porn__ to __Porn and Supanee__ . Begin the paragraph this way:
Porn and Supanee are refugees from Thailand. I am responsible for them.

WRITING ACTIVITY   Tell about someone who is helping you go to school.

22

A Truck

Tom and I have a truck. We bought it last year. We paid $16,000 for it. We need it for our business. We use it every day to deliver packages. We take good care of it because our business depends on it.

Change the title to __Two Trucks__ . Begin the paragraph this way:
Tom and I have two trucks. We bought them . . .

WRITING ACTIVITY   Tell about something you own that helps you with your job or in school. Explain why it is important to you.

23

The Math Class

I don't like my math class. I can't understand my math book. I can't understand my teacher, either. My classmates are unfriendly. My teacher is boring. I fail all my tests. I want to change my class.

Change __I__ to __Carmen and I__ . Begin the paragraph this way:
__Carmen and I don't like our math class. We . . .__

WRITING ACTIVITY   Tell about a class you don't (didn't) like. Tell why.

24

Going Back

Elizabeth is not happy with her life. She is here in this country alone. She misses her family and friends. She wants to go back to her native country to be with her family again. She feels that she will be happier living with her family. Elizabeth is planning to quit her job and use her money to buy a plane ticket.

Change __Elizabeth__ to __Charles__ . Begin the paragraph this way:
__Charles is not happy with his life.__

WRITING ACTIVITY   Tell about someone who wants to go back to her/his native country. Explain the reasons.

25

A Child's Pain

Janet is six years old. She lives with her mother because her mother and father are separated. Janet loves her mother, but she loves her father, too. Every day she asks her mother when "daddy" is coming home. She misses her father very much.

Change **Janet** to **Danny** . Begin the paragraph this way:
 Danny is six years old. He lives with his . . .

WRITING ACTIVITY   Tell about a child whose parents do not (did not) live together. Describe the child's feelings.

26

Making Progress

Raymond is not satisfied with his progress. He thinks that his grades are too low. He studies a lot, and he does all his homework. He attends all his classes. But when Raymond gets his grade report at the end of each semester, his grades are all B's and C's. He wants all A's. What do you think of his situation?

Change **Raymond** to **Yolanda** . Begin the paragraph this way:
 Yolanda is not satisfied with her progress.

WRITING ACTIVITY   Why do you think Raymond is getting B's and C's instead of A's. What can he do to improve his grades?

27

A Loving Nephew

Peter loves his Aunt Mary. He visits her every Sunday. He always brings her a cake or some donuts. He asks her how she is feeling. Peter spends several hours talking with her. Then he cooks dinner for her and eats with her. After dinner Peter says goodbye to her and goes home. He promises her that he will come to see her the following Sunday.

Change __Aunt Mary__ to __Uncle Fred__ . Begin the paragraph this way:
__Peter loves his Uncle Fred. He visits him . . .__

WRITING ACTIVITY   Tell about an older relative or friend that you visit. Tell what you do for this person.

28

The Soup Kitchen

I work in a soup kitchen as a volunteer. The cooks prepare the soup, and I talk with the old people outside. Many of them wait in line for soup every day. They need the soup kitchen because they are poor. At 1:00 the soup is ready. I fill a big bowl with soup for each person. When the people finish, I wash the dishes and clean the kitchen for the next day. I like the soup kitchen.

Change the paragraph to the past tense. Begin the paragraph this way:
__Last year I worked in a soup kitchen . . .__

WRITING ACTIVITY   Do you volunteer to help people in your community? Tell what you do now or could do in the future?

29

Summer School

Every summer the teachers attend classes at the university. They need to learn more about their profession. They want to become better teachers. They study hard. They share their classroom experiences with each other. The teachers learn a lot in six weeks. In September they return to their schools better prepared to teach their students.

Change the paragraph to the past tense. Begin the paragraph this way:

Last summer the teachers attended . . .

WRITING ACTIVITY   Think about a good teacher you had in the past. Tell why that teacher was good.

30

The Super

The super did his job very well yesterday. He cleaned all the stairs in the building. He mopped all the floors. He repaired the lobby door. He replaced some light bulbs in the hallways. He took out all the garbage. He fixed the sink in Mrs. Dolan's apartment. Yesterday the super made the landlord and the tenants very happy.

Change the paragraph to the negative. Begin the paragraph this way:

The super didn't do his job very well . . .

WRITING ACTIVITY   Did your super or janitor do a good job last week? Explain.

31

The Promise

Our mother kept her promise to her family. She listened to our advice. She stopped drinking. She started attending A.A. meetings. She threw out all the liquor in the house. She began to believe in herself. She began to feel happy. We became a real family again.

Change the paragraph to the negative. Begin the paragraph this way:

Our mother didn't keep her promise . . .

WRITING ACTIVITY   Tell about a friend or relative who promised to change his/her life. What happened?

32

Aunt Lucy

Aunt Lucy is my favorite aunt. I am always in her house. She is happy when I am with her because she is alone in her house. She is divorced and her only child, Henry, is married. She is very kind to me. She is always helping me with my problems. She is like a mother to me.

Change the paragraph to the past tense. Begin the paragraph this way:

When I was a child, Aunt Lucy was . . .

WRITING ACTIVITY   Tell about a relative who was very good to you when you were a child.

33

The Mountain Village

Our village is located in the mountains. It is a beautiful village. The houses are white with red roofs. Everyone is poor but happy. The village square is full of people in the evenings. The church is full of people on Sundays. The village is the center of our lives.

Change the paragraph to the past tense. Begin the paragraph this way:

Before the earthquake, our village was located in the mountains.

WRITING ACTIVITY   Describe a village or city in your native country. Tell about the buildings, streets, people. Are there mountains or rivers? Is there an ocean? What do people do during the day, in the evening, on weekends?

34

Juvenile Delinquents

Harry and Carlos are juvenile delinquents. They are members of a gang. They are in the streets all the time. They are often drunk and are often in trouble with the police. Their friends are the same way. It is a real shame.

Change the paragraph to the past tense. Begin the paragraph this way:

Before Harry and Carlos went into the army, they were juvenile delinquents.

WRITING ACTIVITY   Tell about a teenager who has problems. What can parents, relatives, friends, or the government do to help this person? How can the person help himself/herself?

35

A Good Time

Every summer my parents send me to camp. They buy clothes and equipment for me and give me some extra money. They bring me to the camp and leave me with the counselor. Then they forget about me for the whole summer. They take a vacation and have a good time together. They think that I have a good time by myself.

Change Every summer to Last summer and change the paragraph to the past tense. Begin the paragraph this way:

Last summer my parents sent me to camp.

WRITING ACTIVITY   Did your parents ever send you away from home? (To camp? To school? To live with a relative?) Explain how you felt.

36

Mistakes

When I do something wrong or when I make a mistake, I feel bad. I feel ashamed. I think that I am stupid. I get angry at myself. I lose my self-respect. I forget that I am only human.

Change the paragraph to the past tense. Begin the paragraph this way:

Many years ago, when I did something . . .

WRITING ACTIVITY   Tell about a mistake that you made. What did you do to correct the mistake?

37

Concentration

When I am studying, I can't do anything else at the same time. I can't listen to music. I can't watch television. I can't talk to anyone. I can't study in a noisy place. I can only study in the library at school or in my bedroom at home where I can have peace. I can't concentrate when there are distractions all around me.

Change the paragraph to the past tense. Begin the paragraph this way:

Last year when I was studying, I couldn't do anything else at the . . .

WRITING ACTIVITY   Tell how you study for school. Do you study at home? In the library? In a friend's house? Do you study alone? With a friend? With a tutor? While you study, do you listen to music? Watch TV? Eat?

38

A Vocation

I am in Guatemala. I live in a small village. I live with three other women. We help the people in the village. We teach nutrition and child care. We work very hard and we get very little money. We do everything for God and for the people.

Change the paragraph to the future tense. Begin the paragraph this way:

Next year I will be in Guatemala. I will live . . .

WRITING ACTIVITY   Tell about someone who is helping people in this country or in another country.

39

Winter in the Mountains

Every year winter comes to the mountains early. The days and nights get very cold. The trees lose all their leaves. The lakes freeze. Snow and ice cover everything. The winds blow hard through the mountains and valleys. Animals try to find food under the snow. People stay inside to keep warm. They wait for the long winter months to pass.

Change the paragraph to the future tense. Begin the paragraph this way:

Next year winter will come to the . . .

WRITING ACTIVITY   Describe winter in the city. Tell what people do to keep comfortable. Are there special problems in the winter? Explain.

40

A Change for the Better

I will change my life. I will become a different person. I will love my family and friends more. I will be more considerate. I will help other people. I will try to be more generous. I will not think of myself first all the time. I will not be so selfish.

Change the paragraph to the *going to* future. Begin the paragraph this way:

I am going to change my life.

WRITING ACTIVITY   Tell how you will change your life to become a better, happier person.

41

Thinking Positively

I will change my attitude about myself. I will not be so negative about myself. I will not think that I am "no good." I will accept myself as I am. I will appreciate myself more. I will believe that I am an important person in this world. I will treat myself very well.

Change the paragraph to the *going to* future. Begin the paragraph this way:

I am going to change my attitude about myself.

WRITING ACTIVITY   Tell what you like and don't like about yourself. Can you change the things you don't like? Explain.

42

Spring

Soon the snow and ice will disappear. The sun will shine brightly in the sky. The birds will return. The flowers and the grass will grow. The leaves will appear on the trees. Old people will sit in the park in the warm sun. Children will play outside after school. We will hear happy sounds in the air once again. We will feel full of new life.

Change the paragraph to the *going to* future. Begin the paragraph this way:

Soon the snow and ice are going to disappear.

WRITING ACTIVITY   Tell about the seasons in your native country. Are they the same as, or different from, the seasons in this country?

43

Letting Go

Some day my son will meet the right woman. He will fall in love with this woman. Then he will marry her. He will move out of my house. He will live with her. My son will leave me all alone. He will forget about me. He will think only about her.

Change the paragraph to the *going to* future. Begin the paragraph this way:

Some day my son is going to meet the . . .

WRITING ACTIVITY   *If you are married*, tell about your relationship with your mother or father. How often do you see them, write to them, or call them? Explain. **OR** *When you get married*, will you have a good relationship with your mother or father? Tell what you will do.

44

The Street Below

In the summer I often watch the action on the street below my apartment. The neighborhood boys play stickball. The girls jump rope. Some of the men fix their cars. Others stand on the corner and drink beer. The women talk about their families. Some teenagers listen to music on the sidewalk. All of them, young and old, enjoy the fresh air outdoors.

Change the first sentence to:

Right now I am watching the action . . .

Write the paragraph again.

WRITING ACTIVITY   Describe what is happening in your neighborhood right now. **OR** Tell about a typical day in your neighborhood.

45

A Loving Father

My father holds me close. He kisses me on my cheek. He smiles at me. He tells me that I am his favorite child. I look into his beautiful eyes to find the truth. I laugh. I cry. I feel so happy now.

Change the first sentence to:

My father is holding me close.

Write the paragraph again.

WRITING ACTIVITY   Tell how you feel about your father or mother now or how you felt when you were a child.

Grammar Pages

Subject Pronouns

		Examples:
I	*We*	1. *Mary* is a good friend. *She* listens to my problems.
You	*You*	2. *Peter* is a good friend. *He* listens to my problems.
		3. *Mary and Peter* are good friends. *They* listen to my problems.
He	*They*	4. *The truck* is expensive. *It* costs a lot of money.
She		5. *The trucks* are expensive. *They* cost a lot of money.
It		

PRACTICE   *Use the appropriate subject pronouns.*

Example: *Margaret* is my cousin. *She* is coming to visit me soon.
(Change *Margaret* to *William* and write the sentence again.)

William is my cousin. He is coming to visit me soon.

1. *Nancy* is sick today. *She* will not be in school.
   (Change *Nancy* to *John* and write the sentence again.)

_____

2. *Edward* has a new car. *He* likes it very much.
   (Change *Edward* to *Helen* and write the sentence again.)

_____

3. *Mrs. Johnson* can't speak Spanish well. *She* would like to learn.
   (Change *Mrs. Johnson* to *Mr. and Mrs. Johnson* and write the sentence again.)

_____

4. *The washing machine* broke down. *It* won't work properly.
   (Change *the washing machine* to *the washing machines* and write the sentence again.)

_____

5. *Margaret* works in a day care center. *She* likes children.
   (Change *Margaret* to *Luis* and write the sentence again.)

_____

6. *My husband* can't come today. *He* will come tomorrow.
   (Change *My husband* to *My husband and I* and write the sentence again.)

_____

7. *David* lives alone. *He* prefers it that way.
   (Change *David* to *Susan* and write the sentence again.)

_____

8. *Mary* needs a bigger apartment. *She* is planning to move.
   (Change *Mary* to *Richard* and write the sentence again.)

_____

Present Tense of *to be*

		Examples:
I am	*(I'm)*	1. *I am* a good student.
You are	*(You're)*	2. *You are* my best friend.
He is	*(He's)*	3. *He is* a taxi driver.
She is	*(She's)*	4. *She is* my favorite cousin.
It is	*(It's)*	5. *It is* very cold outside.
We are	*(We're)*	6. *We are* in the living room.
You are	*(You're)*	7. *You are* all doing well.
They are	*(They're)*	8. *They are* very happy.

PRACTICE *Use the appropriate form of* **be.**

Example: I am an intelligent student.
(Change *I* to *He* and write the sentence again.)

He is an intelligent student.

1. *I* am in love with Henry.
   (Change *I* to *She* and write the sentence again.)

   _____

2. *It* is in very bad condition.
   (Change *It* to *They* and write the sentence again.)

   _____

3. *They* are downstairs in the basement.
   (Change *They* to *He* and write the sentence again.)

   _____

4. *I* am an interesting person.
   (Change *I* to *You* and write the sentence again.)

   _____

5. *She* is in the cafeteria.
   (Change *She* to *They* and write the sentence again.)

   _____

6. *They* are on top of the refrigerator.
   (Change *They* to *It* and write the sentence again.)

   _____

7. *I* am in a hurry today.
   (Change *I* to *We* and write the sentence again.)

   _____

8. *He* is at the airport.
   (Change *He* to *They* and write the sentence again.)

   _____

Present Tense of *to be* (Negative)

		Examples:
I am not	*We are not (aren't)*	1. I *am not* ready yet.
You are not (aren't)	*You are not (aren't)*	2. You *are not* responsible for the accident.
He is not (isn't)		3. He *is not* a happy person.
She is not (isn't)	*They are not (aren't)*	4. She *is not* home right now.
It is not (isn't)		5. It *is not* a good car.

Examples:
1. I *am not* ready yet.
2. You *are not* responsible for the accident.
3. He *is not* a happy person.
4. She *is not* home right now.
5. It *is not* a good car.
6. We *are not* in the right place.
7. All of you *are not* sure of the answer.
8. They *are not* in the bedroom.

PRACTICE   *Change each sentence to make it negative.*

Example: I *am* very nervous.

   I am not very nervous.

1. He *is* the next in line.

_____

2. It *is* a good idea.

_____

3. I *am* happy with the results.

_____

4. We *are* ready for the test.

_____

5. They *are* good people.

_____

6. She *is* in college.

_____

7. I *am* in a good mood.

_____

8. He *is* an interesting speaker.

_____

9. We *are* tired of studying.

_____

10. She *is* in her bedroom.

_____

Object Pronouns

me	*us*
you	*you*
him	
her	*them*
it	

Examples:
1. *I* have something to tell you. Please call *me* tonight.
2. When *you* need help, I will help *you*.
3. *John* is my son. I love *him* very much.
4. *Sarah* is my daughter. I love *her* very much.
5. Where is the *knife?* I need *it* now.
6. *We* need some money. Please lend *us* $20.
7. *John and Sarah* are my children. I love *them* very much.

PRACTICE   *Use the appropriate object noun.*

Example: *Danny* has a problem. I need to talk to *him* about it.
(Change *Danny* to *Maria* and write the sentence again.)

   Maria has a problem. I need to talk to her about it.

1. My *son* is sick. I need to take *him* to the doctor.
   (Change *son* to *daughter* and write the sentence again.)

   _____

2. My *aunt* lives near me. I see *her* often.
   (Change *aunt* to *uncle* and write the sentence again.)

   _____

3. Someone broke the *chair*. Can you fix *it?*
   (Change *chair* to *chairs* and write the sentence again.)

   _____

4. *Teresa* can't speak English. Can you teach *her?*
   (Change *Teresa* to *Teresa and Alice* and write the sentence again.)

   _____

5. *Thomas* can't speak English. Can you teach *him?*
   (Change *Thomas* to *Thomas and José* and write the sentence again.)

   _____

6. *I* don't know the answer. Can you tell *me* the answer?
   (Change *I* to *We* and write the sentence again.)

   _____

7. *Fred* needs to talk to you. Will you call *him?*
   (Change *Fred* to *Maria* and write the sentence again.)

   _____

8. *Alice* needs a roommate. I plan to move in with *her*.
   (Change *Alice* to *Edward* and write the sentence again.)

   _____

Possessive Adjectives

my	our
your	your
his	
her	their
its	

Examples:
1. *I* love *my* children very much.
2. *You* need to take *your* medicine every day.
3. *He* calls *his* mother every week.
4. *She* visits *her* father on Sundays.
5. *The sun* gives *its* light each day.
6. *We* like *our* neighborhood.
7. All of *you* need to do *your* homework.
8. *They* live with *their* parents.

PRACTICE   *Use the appropriate possessive adjective.*

Example: *Stephen* studies in *his* bedroom.
(Change *Stephen* to *Nancy* and write the sentence again.)

Nancy studies in her bedroom.

1. *Bob* likes *his* job.
   (Change *Bob* to *Jennifer* and write the sentence again.)

   _____

2. *Sheila* plays with *her* friend every day after school.
   (Change *Sheila* to *Freddy* and write the sentence again.)

   _____

3. *I* plan to send *my* children to college.
   (Change *I* to *My wife and I* and write the sentence again.)

   _____

4. *I* need to think about *my* future.
   (Change *I* to *You* and write the sentence again.)

   _____

5. *Marilyn* can understand *her* teacher well.
   (Change *Marilyn* to *The students* and write the sentence again.)

   _____

6. *Evelyn* has to find a solution to *her* problem.
   (Change *Evelyn* to *Paul* and write the sentence again.)

   _____

7. *Manuel* doesn't like *his* neighbors.
   (Change *Manuel* to *Margaret* and write the sentence again.)

   _____

8. *Mrs. Martinez* can't understand *her* children.
   (Change *Mrs. Martinez* to *Many mothers* and write the sentence again.)

   _____

Present Tense Negative

		Examples:
I don't live	We don't live	1. I *don't drink* alcohol.
You don't live	You don't live	2. You *don't love* me anymore.
He doesn't live		3. He *doesn't have* a nice personality.
She doesn't live	They don't live	4. She *doesn't know* the answer to your question.
It doesn't live		5. It *doesn't work* right.
		6. We *don't like* rap music.
		7. All of you *don't study* enough.
		8. They *don't want* any more soda.

PRACTICE   *Change each sentence to make it negative.*

Example: I *have* a lot of time to study.

I don't have a lot of time to study.

Patricia *works on* weekends.

Patricia doesn't work on weekends.

1. We *need* a bigger apartment.

_____

2. Edward *speaks* English well.

_____

3. Carmen *knows* all of her classmates.

_____

4. I *run* every morning in the park.

_____

5. Andy *has* two dogs.

_____

6. Maria *lives* with her sister.

_____

7. I *plan* to move soon.

_____

8. Jennifer *makes* her bed every morning.

_____

9. We *eat* healthy food.

_____

10. They *spend* too much money on clothes.

_____

Present Tense

I live   We live
You live   You live
He lives
She lives   They live
It lives

Examples:
1. I *go* to work at 7:30 in the morning.
2. You *have* beautiful eyes.
3. He *eats* too much.
4. She *has* three children.
5. It *costs* a lot of money.
6. We *think* about you all the time.
7. All of you *need* a lot of practice.
8. They *call* me once a week.

PRACTICE   *Use the appropriate present tense form.*

Example: *Peter and David* work in a factory.
(Change *Peter and David* to *Carlos* and write the sentence again.)

   Carlos works in a factory.

1. *Carol and Susan* live in an apartment.
   (Change *Carol and Susan* to *Rosalyn* and write the sentence again.)

   _____

2. *Mr. and Ms. Martinez* play tennis every Saturday.
   (Change *Mr. and Ms. Martinez* to *Mr. Bradford* and write the sentence again.)

   _____

3. *John* needs some advice.
   (Change *John* to *Michael and Daniel* and write the sentence again.)

   _____

4. *The boys* have a good idea.
   (Change *The boys* to *The boy* and write the sentence again.)

   _____

5. *Ms. Lee* cooks many different kinds of food.
   (Change *Ms. Lee* to *Ms. Tan and Ms. Chiu* and write the sentence again.)

   _____

6. *The workers* want more money.
   (Change *The workers* to *Raymond* and write the sentence again.)

   _____

7. *Women* like to wear the latest fashions.
   (Change *Women* to *Elizabeth* and write the sentence again.)

   _____

8. *Mr. Lewis* plays tennis on weekends.
   (Change *Mr. Lewis* to *Howard and Bill* and write the sentence again.)

   _____

Past Tense of Regular Verbs

		Examples:
I want*ed*	We want*ed*	1. I *asked* the teacher about the homework.
You want*ed*	You want*ed*	2. You *cooked* a delicious dinner.
He want*ed*		3. He *needed* some money.
She want*ed*	They want*ed*	4. She *called* her mother.
It want*ed*		5. It *started* at 8:00.
		6. We *washed* the dishes together.
		7. All of you *finished* your work.
		8. They *walked* to school.

PRACTICE   *Change each sentence to the past tense.*

Example: I *work* in a hospital.

Last year I worked in a hospital.

1. She *lives* with her mother.

   Two years ago _____

2. We *travel* to Puerto Rico.

   Last month _____

3. I *talk* with my friend.

   Last week _____

4. He *cleans* his apartment.

   Yesterday _____

5. They *watch* a good program on T.V.

   Last night _____

6. You *look* nice.

   Yesterday _____

7. He *loves* to play baseball.

   When he was young _____

8. I *open* the window.

   A few minutes ago _____

9. She *enjoys* some good music.

   Last night _____

10. I *play* the piano.

    When I was in high school, _____

Past Tense Negative (*didn't*)

I *didn't need*   We *didn't need*
You *didn't need*   You *didn't need*
He *didn't need*
She *didn't need*   They *didn't need*
It *didn't need*

Examples:
1. I *didn't go* to school yesterday.
2. You *didn't finish* your work.
3. He *didn't like* the movie.
4. She *didn't find* a job.
5. It *didn't work* right.
6. We *didn't move* last year.
7. All of you *didn't pass* the test.
8. They *didn't buy* a new car.

PRACTICE   *Change each sentence to the past tense negative.*

Example: I *needed* a bigger apartment.

I didn't need a bigger apartment.

1. I *watched* television last night.

_____

2. He *wanted* the job.

_____

3. We *cooked* something special yesterday.

_____

4. She *called* her mother last week.

_____

5. They *went* to the movies.

_____

6. I *had* a good time at the party.

_____

7. We *opened* a bank account.

_____

8. I *worked* last Saturday.

_____

9. She *felt* happy yesterday.

_____

10. They *made* many mistakes on the test.

_____

Past Tense of *to be*

		Examples:
I was	*We were*	1. I *was* a teacher from 1980 to 1992.
You were	*You were*	2. You *were* a good student last semester.
He was		3. He *was* absent from school yesterday.
She was	*They were*	4. She *was* very tired last night.
It was		5. It *was* a good movie.

6. We *were* good friends when we *were* children.
7. All of you *were* supposed to do your homework.
8. They *were* nervous when they took the test yesterday.

PRACTICE   *Change each sentence to the past tense.*

Example: I *am* very angry.

Yesterday   I was very angry. _____

1. He *is* in the hospital.

   Last week _____

2. I *am* in the kitchen.

   A few minutes ago _____

3. We *are* in love.

   A few months ago _____

4. She *is* my best friend.

   Last year _____

5. They *are* very happy.

   Last night _____

6. He *is* a drug addict.

   Many years ago _____

7. I *am* in good physical condition.

   When I was younger _____

8. He *is* a guest in my house.

   Last week _____

9. We *are* at our vacation home.

   Last summer _____

10. They *are* afraid to take a chance.

    Last night _____

Past Tense of Irregular Verbs

Base Form	Past Form		Base Form	Past Form		Base Form	Past Form
buy	bought		make	made		go	went
do	did		say	said		have	had
feel	felt		send	sent		leave	left
forget	forgot		speak	spoke		tell	told
get	got		spend	spent		think	thought
give	gave		take	took		wake	woke

Examples:

1. I *felt* very happy yesterday.
2. He *spent* too much money for that car.
3. He *said* that you are a good person.
4. She *had* an appointment at the hospital.

5. It *took* three hours to finish the job.
6. We *left* home at 8:00 A.M.
7. All of you *made* too many mistakes on the exam.
8. They *forgot* to call me.

PRACTICE   *Change each sentence to the past tense.*

Example: I *have* a good time with you.

Last night ___I had a good time with you._____

1. I *buy* milk and bread at the supermarket.

   Yesterday _____

2. She *wakes* up at 6:30.

   This morning _____

3. You *say* the right thing.

   Last night _____

4. They *give* me some money

   Last Saturday _____

5. He *takes* the bus to school.

   Yesterday _____

6. I *do* a lot of things.

   Last Sunday _____

7. He *makes* delicious cookies.

   Last night _____

8. I *leave* my house at 7:30.

   Yesterday morning _____

9. We *speak* to each other honestly.

   Last week _____

10. She *gets* a lot of advice from her father.

    Yesterday _____

167

Couldn't

I couldn't wait	*We couldn't wait*	
You couldn't wait	*You couldn't wait*	
He couldn't wait		
She couldn't wait	*They couldn't wait*	
It couldn't wait		

Examples:
1. I *couldn't call* you last night.
2. You *couldn't do* the job right.
3. He *couldn't understand* the lesson.
4. She *couldn't finish* her homework.
5. It *couldn't be* correct.
6. We *couldn't pay* the rent last month.
7. All of you *couldn't make* so many mistakes.
8. They *couldn't go* to school yesterday.

PRACTICE   *Change each sentence to the past tense negative with* **couldn't.**

Example: I *can't cook* dinner.

Last night ___I couldn't cook dinner._____

1. I *can't speak* English well.

   Last year _____

2. He *can't watch* the television program.

   Last night _____

3. We *can't take* our vacation.

   Last month _____

4. They *can't come* to the party.

   Last Saturday _____

5. She *can't keep* her appointment.

   Yesterday _____

6. You *can't do* the assignment.

   Yesterday _____

7. He *can't listen* to the news on the radio.

   Last night _____

8. I *can't tolerate* his abuse.

   After we were married, _____

9. We *can't arrive* on time for the class.

   Yesterday _____

10. They *can't explain* what happened.

    After the accident, _____

Future Tense (*will*)

I will have   We will have
You will have   You will have
He will have
She will have   They will have
It will have

Examples:
1. I *will see* you tomorrow.
2. You *will have* a wonderful life.
3. He *will marry* a wonderful woman.
4. She *will pass* all her courses.
5. It *will hurt* a little bit.
6. We *will eat* in a restaurant tonight.
7. All of you *will find* a better future someday.
8. They *will need* your help later.

PRACTICE   *Change each sentence to the future tense.*

Example: I *eat* rice and beans.

Tomorrow   I will eat rice and beans. _____

1. I *do* my homework.

 Tonight _____

2. He *runs* in the park.

 Tomorrow _____

3. We *visit* our parents.

 Next week _____

4. They *call* me.

 Tomorrow night _____

5. She *cleans* her apartment.

 Next Saturday _____

6. I *come* early.

 Tomorrow morning _____

7. He *leaves* work at 5:00.

 Tomorrow _____

8. I *walk* my dog.

 Tomorrow night _____

9. She *talks* to her friend.

 Next Sunday _____

10. We *finish* the assignments quickly.

 For the next class _____

Future Tense (*going to*)

I am going to run
You are going to run
He is going to run
She is going to run
It is going to run

We are going to run
You are going to run

They are going to run

Examples:
1. I *am going to eat* fried chicken for dinner.
2. You *are going to have* problems with him.
3. He *is going to get* another job.
4. She *is going to marry* Bruce in June.
5. It *is going to rain* tomorrow.
6. We *are going to pass* this course.
7. All of you *are going to have* fun at the party.
8. They *are going to visit* me next Sunday.

PRACTICE   ***Change each sentence to the future tense using the* going to *form.***

Examples: I *get up* at 7:00.

   I am going to get up at 7:00.

Maria *lives* with her brother.

   Maria is going to live with her brother.

1. I *do* the laundry on Saturday.

   _____

2. Antonio *works* after school next year.

   _____

3. The students *study* in the library every afternoon.

   _____

4. I *cook* for my family tonight.

   _____

5. They *swim* in the lake tomorrow.

   _____

6. Elaine *has* a baby.

   _____

7. I *take* a trip every summer.

   _____

8. She *gets* good grades.

   _____

9. We *need* your help.

   _____

10. They *celebrate* their birthdays together.

   _____

Present Continuous Tense

Examples:

I am eating	*We are eating*	1. I *am thinking* about my best friend.
You are eating	*You are eating*	2. You *are making* too much noise.
He is eating		3. He *is washing* his car.
She is eating	*They are eating*	4. She *is taking* a shower.
It is eating		5. It *is raining*.
		6. We *are watching* T.V.
		7. All of you *are coming* to my wedding.
		8. They *are planning* a party.

PRACTICE *Change each sentence to the present continuous tense.*

Example: I *live* in Miami.

   I am living in Miami.

1. I *drink* milk.

   _____

2. You *work* too hard.

   _____

3. He *plays* baseball.

   _____

4. We *make* too many mistakes.

   _____

5. She *cooks* spaghetti.

   _____

6. They *take* the bus.

   _____

7. I *listen* to the radio.

   _____

8. He *smokes* a pipe.

   _____

9. We *read* the newspaper.

   _____

10. She *goes* to her mother's house.

   _____

SECTION FOUR

Handwriting Practice

Frank's Restaurant

Frank is an Italian chef. He owns a small restaurant near the lake. He cooks everything himself. The food is delicious and the prices are reasonable. He treats his customers well. If you want a good meal, go to Frank's Restaurant. You will not be sorry.

Frank's Restaurant

Frank is an Italian chef. He owns a small restaurant near the lake. He cooks everything himself. The food is delicious and the prices are reasonable. He treats his customers well. If you want a good meal, go to Frank's Restaurant. You will not be sorry.

Example:

Frank is an Italian chef. He owns a . . .

Frank is an Italian chef. He owns a . . .

Mr. Smith's Problem

Mr. Smith is an auto salesman. He sells used cars. He is a trustworthy person, but people don't like to buy used cars from him. He sells big cars. People want to buy small cars. Mr. Smith has to find an answer to his problem soon, or he will go out of business.

Mr. Smith's Problem

Mr. Smith is an auto salesman. He sells used cars. He is a trustworthy person, but people don't like to buy used cars from him. He sells big cars. People want to buy small cars. Mr. Smith has to find an answer to his problem soon, or he will go out of business.

A Different Way

Ms. Armstrong has a different way of teaching math. She uses colored pieces of wood. I think it is a good method. I am learning quickly. I am enjoying class more. Now I feel like an intelligent student in math.

A Different Way

Ms. Armstrong has a different way of teaching math. She uses colored pieces of wood. I think it is a good method. I am learning quickly. I am enjoying class more. Now I feel like an intelligent student in math.

The Homeless Man

There is a vacant building on my block. Nobody lives in it because it is very old. Sometimes I see a poor man go into the building. He sleeps there because he is homeless. The building is an unsafe place to stay, but the man doesn't have any other place to sleep. What can I do to help him?

The Homeless Man

There is a vacant building on my block. Nobody lives in it because it is very old. Sometimes I see a poor man go into the building. He sleeps there because he is homeless. The building is an unsafe place to stay, but the man doesn't have any other place to sleep. What can I do to help him?

The Mountain Village

Our village is located in the mountains. It is a beautiful village. The houses are white with red roofs. Everyone is poor but happy. The village square is full of people in the evenings. The church is full of people on Sundays. The village is the center of our lives.

The Mountain Village

Our village is located in the mountains. It is a beautiful village. The houses are white with red roofs. Everyone is poor but happy. The village square is full of people in the evenings. The church is full of people on Sundays. The village is the center of our lives.

A Great Place to Live?

This city is a great place to live. The air is clean and the streets are quiet. The transportation system is efficient. Food and rent are cheap. It is easy to find a job. People are friendly and helpful. It is safe to go out at night.

A Great Place to Live?

This city is a great place to live. The air is clean and the streets are quiet. The transportation system is efficient. Food and rent are cheap. It is easy to find a job. People are friendly and helpful. It is safe to go out at night.